The Simple Leader

Personal and Professional Leadership
at the Nexus of Lean and Zen

By Kevin L. Meyer

Foreword by Matthew E. May

Dedication

To my parents, who encouraged me to explore and learn, and my wife, Kim, who taught me how to be more empathetic and compassionate.

A special thanks to Matthew May, whose book The Shibumi Strategy *came at just the right time, when I was exploring the application of Zen concepts to personal and professional leadership, helping me regain control over my life.*

Contents

Impressions

I have long felt that Lean thinking and mindfulness are the two most important breakthroughs in recent years to help us sort out increasingly chaotic lives. Practicing Lean thinking is a clear path to professional success in hypercompetitive markets just as practicing mindfulness is the way to wellbeing in adverse conditions. It also turns out that both build on each other, which is what Kevin masterfully demonstrates in this frank, well-written and deeply insightful account of his own journey. *The Simple Leader* is simply a fantastic read!

- Michael Ballé, author of *Lead With Respect: A Novel of Lean Practice*

Leadership is at the core of any organization, and transforming leadership mindsets and practices is at the core of Lean management. Meyer is a rare author who's not only studied Lean deeply but has also served as CEO. *The Simple Leader* is chock full of essential leadership practices that are key to organizational transformation and outstanding business performance alike.

– Karen Martin, author of *The Outstanding Organization: Generate Business Results by Eliminating Chaos and Building the Foundation for Everyday Excellence*

If you're thinking, "Not another book on leadership," then you're in luck. This is not the same old vacuous pablum that so many consultants peddle, or the same sophomoric insights that Zen fanboys wax lyrical over. Kevin's experience as a business CEO, a student of Lean, and a practitioner of Zen combine to produce a uniquely insightful, wonderfully practical guide to management that will be useful to anyone seeking to be a better leader. I defy anyone to read this book and not learn something immediately useful, applicable, and valuable.

- Daniel Markovitz, author of Building the *Fit Organization: Six Core Principles for Making Your Company Stronger, Faster, and More Competitive*

I've always been impressed by Kevin's dedication to simplicity. This book collects his insights from a lifetime of experiences, travel, reading, work and reflection into a simple and practical book. Open up the table of contents and place your finger down on any topic, and I guarantee that you will find practical hints and insights in this book to help you improve. Take a moment to invest in yourself by reading and reflecting on how to reduce complexity in your life and work.

- Jon Miller, author of *Creating a Kaizen Culture: Align the Organization, Achieve Breakthrough Results, and Sustain the Gains*

Lean and Agile thinking are founded in a deep 'Respect for People', experiential learning, and a realization that continuous improvement and innovation come from direct observation at the Gemba. In our increasingly complex, distracted and over stimulated world, presence and mindfulness, captured in the Zen instruction to 'Pay Attention!', are increasingly relevant. This book may not only change how you lead, but also how you live.

- Steve Bell, author of *Run Grow Transform: Integrating Business and Lean IT*

One might say then that Simple, Leader, Lean, and Zen are inherently conflicted, at odds with one another, and that reconciling them would entail a rather Herculean act of creativity. But creativity is the act of bringing something new into existence, the defining quality of which entails connections between seemingly disparate ideas. This is the beauty of *The Simple Leader*. This is power of the Lean-Zen nexus.

- Matthew May, author of *Winning the Brain Game: Fixing the 7 Fatal Flaws of Thinking*

Effective personal leadership, requiring conscious individual reflection, is a critical foundation for effective professional leadership. Building on his deep hands-on experience with core Lean and Zen concepts, principles and practices, Kevin Meyer provides the reader with concrete advice and examples necessary to become that outstanding leader. In The Simple Leader Kevin demonstrates how each of us can gain leadership clarity by reducing leadership strategy and processes down to a handful of important truths. The Simple Leader is a short read that delivers with impact. Read this book.

Adam Zak, co-author of *Simple Excellence: Organizing and Aligning the Management Team in a Lean Transformation*

The simple leader is not simple at all! The simple leader is the one who has tamed complexity with the notion that simplicity is true elegance. The irony is that the more successful we all become, the more we are enveloped by complexity and reject the intelligence of simplicity. The idea that Kevin could succeed in the business world and understand that success is rooted in simplicity is profound. *The Simple Leader* is a fantastic story of how Kevin has done this and I was taken with his honesty and brilliance.

- Paul Akers, author of *Lean Health: Aging in Reverse*

Foreword

Simple. Leader. Lean. Zen.

At first blush, these four words have no obvious or apparent connection. Taken separately, I am certain that they invoke a personal connotation for each of us. Taken together, though, we may be hard pressed conjure up the same level of meaning. To my knowledge, they have never been used together to express a single unified concept.

Until now.

Yet in order for a thinker to devote the kind of enormous time and effort required to conceive and produce a piece of work devoted to the connectedness these four terms, there must be a thread weaving the deeper ideas and philosophies behind them together in such a way that a swatch of fabric we call a book can be created.

There is, and it is Kevin Meyer's great ambition to share that with us in *The Simple Leader*.

Rest assured, it is no easy feat. For me a leader is someone who creates meaningful change. Yet there is nothing simple about creating truly meaningful change, at any level. And the notion of meaningful change is necessarily considered with an eye toward the future. Yet the art of Zen centers on the present, and being present.

Too, the original definition of "Lean thinking" -- as presented their 20-year old book by the same name by James Womack and Daniel Jones -- holds the concept of perfection at its core, the fifth of five key principles. Yet in the Zen view, the concept of perfection is complex rather than simple in meaning, and not at all of the brand advanced in Lean thinking.

One might say then that Simple, Leader, Lean, and Zen are inherently conflicted, at odds with one another, and that reconciling them would entail a rather Herculean act of creativity. But creativity is the act of bringing something new into existence, the defining quality of which entails connections between seemingly disparate ideas.

This is the beauty of *The Simple Leader*. This is power of the Lean-Zen nexus. And this Kevin Meyer's gift to all of us.

We would be well advised to honor it with the intention by which it was bestowed.

Matthew E. May
Spring 2016

Introduction

One day I will find the right words, and they will be simple.
- Jack Kerouac

The first two decades of my career followed the traditional path of a newly-minted engineer. I started out in entry-level roles in R&D and manufacturing, moved up into supervisory roles, and eventually into the management of increasingly large engineering and operations groups. Along the way, I learned how to operate in complex companies and organizations with a variety of bureaucracies and personalities. As I gained experience, I worked in several different locations and industries, bouncing from Boston to Kentucky to Puerto Rico, back to Boston, then eventually to Silicon Valley. I started in food products, switched to making light bulbs, and then eventually found a passion for the medical device industry.

In 1997, my first plant-level leadership position took me to Salt Lake City and came with a hidden surprise: sixty heavy molding presses, operating at full capacity to supply critical downstream factories, but running several months behind schedule. (Lesson: Ask questions during the interview!). Looking for ways to turn around the situation, I searched the nascent Internet and came across the Association for Manufacturing Excellence and was introduced to Lean manufacturing, also known as the Toyota Production System. A few months and a lot of hard work later we caught up, and I was sold on Lean. I didn't realize then how Lean would continue to shape my career and overall life.

Unfortunately, the company was not as enthusiastic about Lean as I was (though they have since become very strong at Lean), so I decided to move to the Central Coast of California and take a great position in the hyper-growth telecom equipment space. Little did I know, the entire industry would rapidly melt down a year later. When it did, I had to shut down an entire facility and lay off a couple hundred brilliant friends—on September 10th, 2001, no less! What a week!

After closing the plant and including myself in the layoff, I started a contract manufacturing company, began doing some Lean consulting, and eventually found my way back into a "real" job as president of a medical device company. Consulting was interesting, but I simply loved transforming real organizations and making real things too much to stay away.

In my new job, life was pretty good. I worked for a great company, had many fun side projects, was a partner in a couple of startups, and a board member in a couple others. I was surrounded by new projects and wild ideas—an engineer's dream come true. What's more, I got to live and play on the beautiful Central Coast of California. I worked hard but I also played hard, having already begun the shift away from describing wealth in material terms while realizing the value of peace, love, and physical and mental exploration. My work life and personal life were in good balance with each other.

Then, out of nowhere, life took a nasty turn. A family medical situation exploded into unpredictable chaos, creating unbelievable amounts of stress that severely impacted both the personal and professional sides of my life. Even my closest friends and family have no idea how close I was to hanging it all up and disappearing to live on a beach in Samoa. Seriously—I had even researched one-way tickets and visa requirements.

Though the temptation to escape was strong, I wasn't willing to give up my professional responsibilities, as they provided a needed break from the difficulties in my personal life. But something had to change. One day, while sitting alone on Anaeho'omalu Beach on the Big Island of Hawaii, it finally dawned on me that balance can be created by focusing on simplification and understanding what is truly important. (I didn't know it at the time, but the act of sitting alone on a beach was important in itself. It combined both *seijaku*, or quietude, and *datsuzoku*, a break from the routine.) I realized that several Lean concepts I had used in manufacturing could be applied to simplify my personal life. At the same time, I also recognized how several Zen concepts I was exploring in my personal life could be applied to simplify my professional life.

After a few years, the family medical situation improved and became manageable, but I continued to explore and further define how Lean and Zen concepts could be applied to personal and professional leadership. I also dug deeper into the fascinating relationship between the two concepts.

A turning point in developing my new personal and professional leadership philosophy came while I was reading Matthew May's *The Shibumi Strategy*, which coalesced and reinforced several concepts and habits I had developed, especially those regarding how Zen pertained to personal leadership. Finally, over the last several years I've read many articles that align with my thinking on leadership, particularly when related to servant, Lean, or Zen styles. These articles provided examples and methods that I experimented with, many of which I will share in this book.

I know I'm treading into some risky waters by combining Lean and Zen. Lean concepts are often misunderstood and misused, and Zen concepts are still viewed with skepticism, if not outright derision, by many people in the West. This is unfortunate, because if we can put away any preconceived ideas we have about Lean or Zen, we can learn much from both.

Leadership does not have to be complex. Mastering personal leadership first is necessary if you want to master and demonstrate professional leadership, and using a core group of Lean and Zen concepts, you can improve both types. Throughout this book, you will find a lot of practical advice for how to be a better leader. I don't create scholarly theoretical models that are too abstract to be useful. I'm a practitioner, and I prefer to focus on concepts I've developed, tried, and refined in the real world. This book is about sharing what works for me. Hopefully, some of the ideas will help you on your leadership journey.

Kevin Meyer
Morro Bay, California

The Why of
The Simple Leader

I've learned that making a 'living'
is not the same thing as 'making a life'.
– Maya Angelou

A 2011 Gallup poll showed that a third of working adults felt like they were strapped for time. This percentage went up as education and income increased, roughly corresponding to increased professional responsibilities. As perceived lack of time increased, the negative impact on people's personal life also increased dramatically, creating the "imbalance" that so many self-help books try to remediate.

Instead of trying to create a balanced life with existing inputs and outputs, shouldn't we instead look at the root cause of the imbalance and attack it at the source? If we can reduce the inputs by simplifying personal and professional leadership, we can create more time and more focus for our tasks. Creating more time and more focus results in fewer necessary outputs, allowing balance to simply happen. This is what happened on my leadership journey—a journey where I discovered how Lean and Zen concepts can eliminate the unnecessary and create an improved, balanced leadership framework.

My goal with this book is to provide a personal and professional leadership guide for the new or struggling leader that creates balance and efficiency by leveraging the simplicity concepts of Zen and the continuous improvement, problem solving, and respect for people attributes of Lean. *The Simple Leader* is a collection of concepts and ideas I have discovered and developed over time. I do not claim to be the originator of any of them, but by bringing them all together in one place, I hope to make your leadership journey smoother and more successful.

Using this Book

Adapt what is useful, reject what is useless,
and add what is specifically your own.
– Bruce Lee

The Buddha himself famously said, "Be a lamp unto your-selves," telling his students they must test everything he said against their own experience. Just as adopting another organization's best practices without clearly understanding why they exist and the context in which they were implemented will often fail, mindlessly adopting new personal and professional leadership methods can also fail.

As you read this book, think about the concepts in each section and how they might apply to you and your team. Take and use what makes sense, modify it to fit your situation, and leave the rest, perhaps for another day.

The book is organized into eight parts, each with a different purpose:

- **Part One: Fundamentals** – A quick history lesson and exploration of the basics of Lean and Zen.
- **Part Two: Reconnect** – Before doing anything, a leader has to be in touch with her or his inner self.
- **Part Three: Create** – Methods to improve personal productivity to prepare for the work that is coming.
- **Part Four: Lead** – How to engage and lead your team as you begin the improvement journey.

- **Part Five: Clarify** – Clarifying what you and your organization are about, defining the current state and the desired future state, and creating a plan.
- **Part Six: Simplify** – Using your new plan, you can take the first step and simplify your operation within the context of that plan.
- **Part Seven: Improve** – Methods to identify and execute improvement projects within the context of your plan.
- **Part Eight: Grow** – Within ongoing improvement projects in place, it is time to stretch yourself and your organization even further.

If you'd like to dive deeper into some of the concepts used in this book, the Resources section at the back has a list of books I recommend reading. You can also find links to multiple online resources at http://www.TheSimpleLeader.com. There, you'll find links to the same books on Amazon, as well as other online resources, including videos.

Part One - Fundamentals

Start by doing what's necessary; then do what's possible;
and suddenly you are doing the impossible.
– St. Francis of Assisi

Let's first lay some groundwork by learning the history and fundamentals of Lean and Zen.

Key points from this section:

- Always consider the perspective of the customer, which could be you or your team.
- The recent history of Lean stretches back to 1910s inside Henry Ford's automobile assembly operations. Sakichi Toyoda took Ford's ideas to Japan, where Toyota continued to evolve the concept. In the 1990s, Lean became popular in the United States with the publishing of James Womack and Daniel Jones's *The Machine That Changed the World*.
- The two pillars of Lean are "create value through continuous improvement" and "respect for people."
- Zen is not necessarily a religion; rather, it is a human- and present-centered way of life.
- The nexus of Lean and Zen includes awareness through observation, simplicity, balance and harmony, and flow.

Who is the Customer?

The ultimate goal of farming is not the growing of crops, but the cultivation and perfection of human beings. – Masanobu Fukuoka

As we'll discover shortly, a key concept in Lean is creating value from the perspective of the customer. Sometimes, however, it is difficult to determine who the actual customer is. Consider a company that manufactures components for a medical device. Is the customer the patient that ultimately uses the device or the doctor that prescribes it? The hospital that procures it or the company that assembles it? The insurance company that pays for it? How about the employees making a living by manufacturing the component?

The correct answer could be any one of these, depending on the context. With Lean, our initial focus is on the next downstream customer, so for the component manufacturer, the customer would be the company that assembles the device. As organizations move further along in a Lean transformation, though, they look at the value creation process throughout the entire supply chain, from their suppliers to the end customers. The most advanced organizations also include their employees.

For the purposes of this book, I'd like you to think of your team and yourself as the customer. We often focus so much on others that we forget to take care of ourselves.

A Note on Motivation and Habits

In *Drive: The Surprising Truth About What Motivates Us*, Daniel Pink describes the problems with if/then-reward/punishment extrinsic motivation. He argues that the carrot and stick approach that has been central to management for centuries is not effective for complex and creative tasks and objectives. Instead, Pink says, people work better if they have the three core components of intrinsic motivation: autonomy, mastery, and purpose. Finding ways to acquire and convey those components is not just important for how we lead others, but for how we lead ourselves.

A surprisingly small amount of what we do each day—including the decisions we make—is voluntary. According a study at Duke University published in 2006, forty percent of all our actions are based on habit. In other words, our habits have a huge impact on our outcomes in life.

Changing our habits can be difficult though. In *The Power of Habit: Why We Do What We Do in Life and Business*, Charles Duhigg identifies three components of habit: cue, routine, and reward. These three components create a self-reinforcing loop. Duhigg argues that habits cannot be eliminated, only changed or replaced.

One key to changing a habit, he writes, is to identify the cue. Cues fall into five categories: location, time, emotional state, other people, or the immediately preceding action. Duhigg also advises readers to look at what the reward for the habit is. For example, is eating one more cookie really for satisfying your hunger, or is it going to create some other emotional response?

17

Once you understand the cues and rewards that underlie your habits, you can create new routines, tweaking the cues and changing the rewards while satisfying your intrinsic desire.

Discovering Lean

Ten years after graduating from college with a chemical engineering degree, I was doing pretty well. I had progressed up through the engineering ranks at a Fortune 50 medical device company, moved into operations, and was running a business unit responsible for a high-profile drug infusion pump product. Although work consumed much of my life in Silicon Valley, I was able to balance it with friends and recreation. Then I got a call from corporate headquarters asking me if I would like to run a large factory in Salt Lake City. To a young career-oriented guy, it sounded like a great opportunity. I would have my own operation, live in a new city, and take a big step up in the company. Without asking a single question, I said yes. (Soon thereafter, I learned an important lesson about why you ask questions when offered new opportunities. Questions can be good things, and the more you ask before getting yourself into an unknown situation, the better.)

In Salt Lake City, I had to oversee a molding operation with sixty heavy presses running at full tilt, twenty-four hours a day, seven days a week, every day of the year. The plant was already three months behind schedule when I got there, and it was falling further and further behind every day. Additionally, the operation came with some unique extracurricular challenges. It supplied components to some critical downstream plants, which made it very visible in the eyes of executives, who closely monitored our output and put a lot of pressure on us to improve results. If that weren't enough, there were also some questionable "activities" occurring during the night shifts. Soon after arriving, I realized that sleep would be a scarce luxury for a while.

Luckily, I had one huge asset in my favor: a bunch of talented folks equally frustrated with the situation and eager to find solutions. Looking for new ideas, I poked around on the internet and discovered something called "Lean manufacturing," also known as the "Toyota Production System," as well as an organization called the Association for Manufacturing Excellence (AME). AME put me in contact with two of their board members, David Hogg and Dan McDonnell, who helped me analyze the situation and what Lean concepts could be applied. Shortly thereafter, I began collecting and sharing Lean concepts with my staff. (As I studied Lean, I collected many resources that would later turn into a side endeavor called Superfactory.)

As a team, we learned how to describe value from the perspective of the customer and how to focus on flow, reduce inventory, and streamline processes. We experimented and failed often, but our efforts soon led to success. We discovered the concept of the "quick changeover," a method that reduces downtime when preparing the machines to manufacture different parts. This allowed our operators to be much more productive, and after a year, we had caught up and were even finding ways to get rid of antiquated equipment while increasing production. When the new presses that headquarters had purchased to add capacity (spending millions of dollars in the process) finally arrived, we did not even need them. Lean really worked, and in the real world no less.

Seeing our results, my passion for Lean grew rapidly, but the company wasn't at a point in its evolution to fully embrace it. In hindsight, this was a lesson on the importance of executive commitment to the Lean transformation process—great improvements can be made at lower levels, but a true organizational transformation requires a cultural change driven from the top. After a frustrating couple of additional years, I decided to leave this company. (Interestingly, the company is now known for its Lean prowess—perhaps the early efforts by our team did have some residual impact after all.)

In 2000, I moved back to California to run a facility recently purchased by a large telecom equipment manufacturer. When I came on board, the operation had an order backlog of nearly a year, and the long lead times were costing the company significant business. Once again, the pressure was on to improve operations. By implementing Lean methods, our team increased output from $500,000 to $5,000,000 a month in less than six months, using the same floor space, equipment, and people as before. Once again, our Lean transformation efforts were doing great things for the company.

Unfortunately, around the middle of 2001, we began to experience a few order cancellations. Little did we know that this was the edge of the cliff that many technology companies went over later that year. The drop-off came so fast that we were still hiring when we began planning our first layoff. On September 10th, I laid off the entire operations group, including myself (a painful experience, although the events of the next day would put that pain into a different perspective). The remaining operations were consolidated into the corporate facility several hundred miles away (a decidedly non-Lean operation) and our product line was soon shut down, demonstrating that without executive leadership support, Lean transformations are very fragile.

Although the companies I worked for did not believe in Lean, my own confidence with it had grown to the point that instead of looking for a new job, I got together with a couple friends and started a contract manufacturing company. We thought we could leverage the power of Lean to tackle the difficult jobs that no one else wanted. We also thought that since we had such a compelling business model we would have no problem finding business. On the first point, we were correct, but on the second one, not so much. Before having to find customers for myself, I was always somewhat envious of the jet-setting lifestyle of my friends in sales and marketing, never understanding why they were paid so well. My two business partners and I, all operations grunts, learned what selling is all about—the hard way. After three years of basically paying our employees but never ourselves, we decided to admit we had learned our lesson. We shut the company down and went our separate ways.

Even though our contract manufacturing operation did not prosper, my knowledge of Lean continued to pay great dividends. Over the years, the list of Lean resources I had been collecting morphed into one of the largest and most comprehensive websites on Lean (Superfactory.com), bringing me into contact with Lean specialists from around the world. I also joined the AME board of directors. After shuttering our company, I leveraged the wealth of contacts from those activities to join the consulting world. One of the contacts helped me find some contract work at a medical device company a short drive from my home on California's Central Coast. One thing led to another, and I soon found myself as the president of the company, overseeing plants in California and Michigan.

In contrast to my earlier experiences, the long-term vision, commitment, and patience of the owners of my new company provided me the opportunity to try some radical Lean experiments over the eight years I was there. We reorganized the company into value streams, developed incredible teams, and even eliminated budgets. Thanks in large part to Lean improvements, we were successful enough to build a large new facility (in expensive California, no less) during the middle of a recession. We also turned traditional outsourcing thinking on its head by shipping products from California to China and India.

Along the way, I learned many valuable lessons, including how to use many of the same Lean concepts to become personally more productive. Later in this book, I'll be sharing these lessons, from both personal and professional perspectives.

A Short History of Lean

To many people, Lean manufacturing was invented in Japan and is synonymous with the Toyota Production System (TPS). They will tell you that TPS is the manufacturing philosophy that enabled Toyota to effectively conquer the global automobile market by reducing waste and improving quality. While that is true, it is not the whole story. Lean has far deeper roots and broader potential.

Fundamentally, Lean is about creating value and empowering people, not just eliminating waste. It was developed long before Toyota—long before the 20th century, in fact. Some trace the roots of Lean all the way back to the Venice Arsenal in the 1500s, when Venetian shipbuilders could roll complete galley ships off the  production line every hour, a remarkable achievement enabled by several weeks of assembly time being sequenced into a continuous, standardized flow. (The genius that helped the military engineers at the Venice Arsenal was none other than Galileo himself—perhaps the first-ever Lean consultant!)

By 1760, the French were using standardized designs and the interchangeability of parts to facilitate repairs on the battlefield. Eli Whitney refined the concept to build 10,000 muskets for the U.S. government at previously unheard-of low prices. Militaries around the world fine-tuned continuous flow and standardized processes throughout the 1800's. Over time, standardization slowly entered into commercial manufacturing.

In 1910, Henry Ford moved his nascent automobile manufacturing operations into Highland Park, Michigan, which is often called the "birthplace of Lean manufacturing." Ford used continuous flow and standardized processes, coupled with innovative machining practices to enable highly consistent, repetitive assembly. Ford often cited the frugality of Benjamin Franklin as an influence on his own business practices—especially Franklin's advice that avoiding unnecessary costs can be more profitable than increasing sales.

Ford was able to reduce core chassis assembly time from twelve hours to less than three. This reduced the cost of a vehicle to the point where it became affordable to the masses and created the demand that helped build Ford's River Rouge plant, which became the world's largest assembly operation with over 100,000 employees. In 1911, Sakichi Toyoda visited the United States and witnessed Ford's Model T production line. He returned to Japan to apply what he saw on his company's handloom weaving machines.

As Ford and Toyoda were streamlining their operations, others were making parallel improvements in the quality and human factors of manufacturing. In 1906, the Italian Vilfredo Pareto noticed that 80% of the wealth was in the hands of 20% of the population, a ratio he found could be applied to areas beyond economics. J.M. Juran took the Pareto Principle and turned it into a quality control tool that focused on finding and eliminating the most important defects. A few years later, Walter Shewhart invented the control chart, which allowed managers to monitor process variables. Shewhart went on to develop the Plan-Do-Study-Act improvement cycle, which Dr. W. Edwards Deming then altered to create the Plan-Do-Check-Act (PDCA) cycle still in use today

In the early years of twentieth century, efficiency expert Frank Gilbreth advanced the science of management by observing construction and factory workers. He and his wife, Lillian, started a consulting company to teach companies how to be more efficient by reducing human motion during assembly processes. Sakichi Toyoda, having already benefited from Henry Ford's ideas, became an expert at reducing human-induced variability in his factories.

Then came World War II. At the beginning of the war, Consolidated Aircraft in San Diego was able to build one B-24 bomber per day. Ford's Charles Sorensen thought he could improve that rate, and as a result of his efforts, a couple years later the Willow Run plant was able to complete one B-24 per hour.

With almost all of the traditional male factory workforce deployed overseas for the war, the human aspect of manufacturing moved front and center. Training Within Industry (TWI) was born as a method to rapidly and effectively train women to work in the wartime factories. After the war, TWI found its way to Japan even as it faded away in the U.S. (only recently has it returned).

The end of the war saw a divergence in philosophies between the two countries. In the U.S., Ford adopted the GM style of top-down, command-and-control management and effectively abandoned Lean manufacturing. Meanwhile in Japan, Toyota led the acceleration of the development and implementation of Lean methods. The company transitioned from a conglomerate that still included the original loom business to a company focused on the auto market. Taiichi Ohno was promoted to machine shop manager and under his watch, Toyota developed the elimination of waste, and creation of value, concepts. The human side of manufacturing was especially important to Ohno, who transferred increasing amounts of authority and control directly to workers on the shop floor.

After being sent to Japan in 1946 and 1947 by the U.S. War Department to help study agriculture and nutrition, Dr. Deming returned to Japan in the early 1950s to give a series of lectures on statistical quality control, demonstrating that improving quality can reduce cost. Toyota embraced these concepts and embedded them into the Toyota Production System (TPS), leading to Toyota winning the Deming Prize for Quality in 1965. Over several years, Taichi Ohno and Shigeo Shingo continued to refine and improve TPS with the development of pull systems, kanban, and quick changeover methods.

By the early 1970s, the rest of the world was beginning to notice Japan's success, and managers assembled for the first study missions to Japan to see TPS in action. Norman Bodek and Robert Hall published some of the first books in English describing aspects of TPS, and by the mid-1980s, several U.S. companies, notably Danaher, HON, and Jake Brake, were actively trying the "new" concepts.

The term "Lean" was first coined by John Krafcik in his MIT master's thesis on Toyota, and then popularized by James Womack and Daniel Jones in the two books that would finally spread a wider knowledge of TPS: The Machine That Changed the World in 1990 (written with Daniel Roos) and Lean Thinking in 1996. Lean Thinking described the core attributes of Lean as:

- Specify value from the perspective of the customer.
- Define the value stream for a product, then analyze the steps in that stream to determine which are waste and which are value-added.

- Establish continuous flow of products from one operation to the next.
- Create pull between process steps to produce the exact amount of products required (i.e., make to order).
- Drive toward perfection, both in terms of quality and eliminating waste.

Those books, as well as organizations such as the Association for Manufacturing Excellence (AME) and the Lean Enterprise Institute, drove a widespread acceptance of Lean as a path to productivity and profitability. By the year 2000, Lean methods were moving out of manufacturing and into office and administrative environments. The spread of Lean continues today, and currently, Lean healthcare, Lean government, Lean information technology (and Agile software development), and Lean construction are particularly popular.

The Two Pillars

The majority of Lean transformations will fail. Sorry, that's just the sad truth. The reason for this failure rate is because Lean has two fundamental pillars that most organizations don't know about, let alone understand the importance of the second. These two pillars are:

- Create value from the customer's perspective through continuous improvement
- Respect for people

27

Lean actually differs slightly from the traditional Toyota Production System in the first pillar. Most organizations trying to become "Lean" focus on reducing waste while Toyota promotes creating flow. Although the approach is different, the tools are generally the same and the end goal is still to create value from the perspective of the customer. (One danger of the first approach is that focusing only on waste reduction can lead to an emphasis on cost-cutting instead of true improvement.)

In Lean thinking, there are seven primary forms of waste: unnecessary transport, unnecessary inventory, unnecessary motion, waiting, overproduction, overprocessing, and defects. Others add the waste of human potential, where employees are thought of as just a pair of hands instead of a brain with creativity, knowledge, and experience.

These forms of waste are present in manufacturing as well as office and administrative environments. In fact, you can even find them at home. Did you cook too much food for dinner last night? Did you have to wait in line to take a shower? Did you have to search for hours to find a tool in your cluttered garage? All these are types of waste as defined by Lean principles.

Is important to remember that something is only waste if it does not create value from the customer's perspective. Identifying the customer and then looking for waste (and value) from the perspective of the customer is far harder than it sounds. Some activities may appear to be waste for one customer and not another. Is a long commute a waste of time? To some it is, to others it is a valuable time to relax and refocus. To add even more complexity, some forms of waste may even be necessary, such as regulatory paperwork. Another example is advertising, an expenditure that doesn't generally add value for the customer but is necessary to help sustain the business.

Even if a company is good at eliminating waste, it still needs to implement the second pillar—respect for people—if it wants to be successful. Respect for people grew out of Toyota's concept of "autonomation." Autonomation means "automation with a human touch." At Toyota and in TPS, machines aid humans, not vice versa. To this day, when you visit a Toyota factory you will see far more humans than at comparable factories of other automakers. Robots are primarily used in dangerous processes and to lift heavy assemblies.

I have come to believe that respect for people is the most important pillar of Lean. However, because it is the least understood (or accepted), it is often the primary reason why most Lean transformations fail. Companies focus on eliminating waste and do not emphasize having respect for people, which causes the whole system to collapse. People are the core value-creators of a Lean organization, something many companies do not understand. Toyota is known for saying "we develop people before we make cars."

Respect for people takes many forms. First, it aims to create an environment for employees where ideas, knowledge, creativity, and experience are valued. Traditional accounting practices measure the cost of the pair of hands, but do not measure the value of experience and creativity in the brain attached to the pair of hands. The lack of a defined value offset is why traditional accounting drives decisions to move factories to countries with lower labor costs, even if hundreds or thousands of experienced, creative people are replaced by even more people with less knowledge.

Respect for people also applies to customers. Every customer is considered to be very important, and their problems are taken seriously. This is part of why Toyota failed with their series of recalls in 2009 and 2010. Instead of holding to a strong culture of respect for its customers, the company tried to play down the stuck accelerator problem for years before the negative perception and press became too great. Imagine how much different those years—and the resulting financial and reputational costs—would have been if Toyota had publicly treated each incident as being extremely serious.

Respect should also be promoted among a company's suppliers and community, which is why a more accurate translation of Toyota's "respect for people" is really "respect for humanity." Engaging the entire value stream and business environment in continuous improvement efforts and knowledge development can pay huge rewards in terms of trust, ideas, and support.

Lean's reputation is not always one of having respect for people. When Womack and Jones wrote their book in 1990, they could not have anticipated the problems associated with "Lean" rhyming with "mean." Not a day goes by without some reference to a "Lean and mean" organization. This is a misperception. Real Lean is definitely not mean to the people implementing it.

Real Lean companies leverage productivity improvements to capture new business, which allows them to keep the people impacted by those improvements. Some Lean companies go so far as to pledge that there will be no layoffs due to Lean efforts. This is often necessary to get buy-in for what can appear to be job-threatening improvement programs. And Lean companies like Toyota are generally not unionized simply because the employees are already treated with respect and often paid better than at comparable organizations.

At its most fundamental level, Lean is about enabling people to create improvements that add value for the customer. Leadership is also about people, including ourselves. Together, this is the foundation for our exploration of how Lean can help transform personal and professional leadership.

Core Lean Tools

One of the attributes that managers and consultants like about Lean is that it has a plethora of tools and methods. Some are more useful than others, and some are straightforward, while others have nonsensical acronyms. Here are the core tools that we'll use later on in this book.

Kaizen: The term means "to take apart" (kai) and "to make good" (zen), and is at the heart of continuous improvement efforts to reduce waste. The Kaizen Event has been popularized by multitudes of consultants who believe a week is the optimal time period to create a single significant change. Hogwash! As long as you thoroughly understand an organization's current conditions and then develop, implement, and test improvements, you can create meaningful change over any period of time. (A week is most likely said to be the optimum time because it lets consultants be home on the weekends.)

Value Stream Map: A flowchart that shows the sequence of steps in a process, from which you can identify wasteful and value-added steps. Typically, 75% of the steps in a process are waste (remember, you are looking at it from the perspective of the customer, not what you think needs to take place).

Flow or Just In Time (JIT): Aligning and balancing the sequence of value-creating process steps to reduce inventory and create steady activity and throughput that is matched to customer demand.

5S: Five S refers to the English terms for the five steps of workplace organization: sort, straighten, sweep, shine, and sustain. By organizing the workplace, you reduce inventory and thereby required space. You also reduce the time it takes to find tools and parts. Organized workplaces are also safer, so some companies add safety as a sixth "S."

Quick Changeover and Set-up Reduction: Reducing the time it takes to set up and change from one process to another by analyzing and reordering activities. Quick changeover was the first tool we implemented to get the medical device molding operation under control and back on schedule.

Standard Work: A very well-defined sequence of activities required to complete a process. For a shop floor operator, this can be the sequence of adding components to an assembly. For a manager, this can be the specific metrics to be reviewed. For someone at home, this can be the morning get-ready-for-work routine.

Go to the Gemba and Genchi Genbutsu: The term "gemba" means "the source." In Lean terms, the gemba is where value is being created—the factory floor, a certain office process, or even in your kitchen at home. Genchi genbutsu translates as "go and see." Lean stresses the idea that you should "see for yourself," i.e., go to the gemba and see what is really going on. You cannot get all the facts and make the right decisions by sitting in a conference room away from the action.

Visual Management and Control: When you walk into a Lean factory, the first thing you see are lots of whiteboards and signs with metrics and status information. Team members are creating charts detailing rejects, capturing improvement ideas on flipcharts, and identifying processes by signs. Information truly is power, so giving workers more information enables them, creating respect for people.

Hoshin Kanri: In its simplest form, hoshin kanri is a method to align long-term strategies with intermediate-term objectives and short-term improvement programs. Many Lean organizations link hoshin kanri into strategic planning activities. We'll talk much more about this later.

Mistake-Proofing or Poka-Yoke: Creating methods that prevent errors from occurring in the first place. A simple example is the USB port that is mechanically designed so the USB device can only be inserted one way.

Those are the core tools of Lean. Unfortunately, many organizations become "tool heads," focusing on implementing the tools without understanding why. All of the tools can create improvements, but first you need to ask what problem you are trying to solve. Then, and only then, should you identify the most appropriate tool.

To compound the difficulty of choosing the right tool,

many Lean tools are counterintuitive (e.g., one-piece flow being more efficient that batch processing). For example, if you had to send out a couple hundred Christmas letters, would you address one envelope, insert the letter, seal the envelope, and add the stamp before moving on to the next one? Or would you address all of the envelopes at once before inserting all the letters, etc.? Guess which process is faster with less chance for errors? Completing an entire stamped, addressed envelope with a letter, one at a time, is faster. Try it sometime.

Discovering Zen

Zen is not some kind of excitement, but concentration on our usual everyday routine. – Shunryu Suzuki

In many respects, my discovery of Zen paralleled my discovery of Lean. For the first decade or so after college, I threw myself headlong into my career and the rewards that came from it—long hours, good pay, and fun toys. It seemed like a pretty good life and I looked forward to where it was headed. I was able to have a fairly good work-life balance that allowed me to take a couple long vacations a year and maintain a solid network of friends and family.

Then life took a couple of unexpected turns. Both happened while I was attempting to turn around the large molding operation in Utah. First, I met and eventually married my lovely wife. Second, the sideline activities resulting from my exploration of Lean, including overseeing websites and being on the boards of industry associations, began to grow. The result was that most of my free time disappeared.

The loss of free time crept up on me almost imperceptibly, and only became evident after moving back to California when a family member began to have significant, often unpredictable, medical issues that I had to manage. My free time no longer existed, and my stress level shot up. Soon, I was dangerously close to cracking—emotionally, physically, and mentally. Very few people realized how close I was to hanging it all up, flying to an empty beach on Samoa, and just living incognito for a while.

Then, one Thursday afternoon, I did crack, but I didn't buy a one-way ticket to Samoa. Instead, I flew myself to my favorite beach in Hawaii that very evening. I spent the next three days by myself. Each day, I would wake up and go to the pool, turn on the laptop and catch up on emails and projects. When the laptop battery died, I'd take it back inside and head to the beach for a couple hours while it charged. I repeated this process throughout the day, until it was time for a caipirinha or glass of Malbec at sunset, followed by more work back in my room until midnight or so.

I returned to the mainland refreshed, caught up, and feeling centered, so after a few months, I did it again. And again, and again. My wife was very supportive, since she could see the positive impact. (There was one interesting dynamic: all of her female friends began asking what was wrong with our marriage, while all of my male friends wanted to know my secret for getting away with such audacity. Vive la différence!) The impact was noticeable to others besides my wife too. The owners of the company

I was running at the time also fully supported my last-minute excursions, and would sometimes even send an email to my staff admonishing them to leave me alone for a few days. I discovered this after probing into why my work-related email volume dropped off suddenly when I escaped.

After a few such trips, I began to realize that the key reason they worked, why they de-stressed and rebalanced my psyche, was not that I got caught up on my tasks, rather that I got away from them. For a few days, I was in control again, I was close to nature, I was living simply. The beach has always been special to me (my wife was born in Hawaii and we were married there), and I found that a couple hours spent sitting alone on a beach had a tremendous rebalancing effect. The time gave me solitude and quietude. And yes,  heightened productivity. On the plane over, I would make a prioritized list of projects I wanted to accomplish, and I would nail them once my mind was cleared.

Back home, I soon discovered that I could achieve a similar "mini-escape" of solitude and quietude on my commute. Fortunately, my commute was much different than what most people would expect in California. Instead of ten lanes of bumper-to-bumper traffic, I drove up the gorgeous Pacific Coast Highway a few miles, then inland on a winding road past avocado and lemon orchards, and finally through several of the vineyards that dot this very unpopulated part of the state. Many days I would see just one or two cars.

Most of the time, I would drive with the radio off, alone with my thoughts. I contemplated problems, but more importantly, I planned my entire day as I was driving. On the drive home in the afternoon, I reflected on the day's events. Over time, I turned the commute into a form of meditation practice (including a period of giving thanks, which does wonders to create a positive frame of mind for the day). Interestingly, I am now unable to listen to books on CD or podcasts in the car because my mind immediately tunes them out and creates silence. My subconscious recognizes the healing power of quietude.

During this time, as I learned how to clear my mind from distractions, I also learned it was okay to give up some control over my circumstances. The unpredictable chaos of the medical situation made it impossible to plan more than a couple days in advance, a direct affront to my engineering-driven mindset. For years I fought to create control, often by micromanaging and creating backup plan after backup plan.

I learned that I simply could not control every possible outcome of every problem, no matter how hard I tried. So, I came up with a new mindset: Don't think so much about tomorrow, let alone waste tremendous amounts of time on layers of contingency plans. Live in the moment. Make decisions based on what is best now, and if something goes south, then and only then do something about it.

Just before the stress situation peaked and I began my

Hawaiian escapes, my wife and I had been thinking about moving to a new house. Our existing house was more than large enough— it had a unique and pleasant design and was located right on California's Central Coast, with views of the ocean to boot. Why move? Because that's what people did, at least before the housing bust. The bigger the better, right? We found a beautiful Asian-inspired house surrounded by vineyards that was exactly our style, except that it was twice as large and more than twice the price of the home we had. We set a maximum limit, placed an offer and countered a couple times, but then we realized we had set the limit for a reason. We ended up losing it.

To tell the truth, we were more relieved than disappointed, especially now, looking back and realizing that we would have bought and leveraged ourselves at the peak of the market. I still shudder to think about how different our lives would have been if we had ended up underwater, owing more money than our home was worth and staring at a huge mortgage payment. I honestly consider our fortune one of the cases of divine intervention in my life. It really feels that way.

Losing the house didn't just create a feeling of relief, it also prompted us to question our motives. Why did we need something larger? We didn't. In fact, perhaps we should have been looking for something smaller. That realization was transformative, and launched our ongoing effort to get rid of excess "stuff" in our lives. We went through the house, throwing out extra, expiring (or expired!) food in the pantry, books we'd never read again, clothes we hadn't worn since the '90s. Once we started, the feeling of liberation, of simplicity, was infectious.

This is how I gained a better awareness of being present in the moment, as well as an awareness of simplicity and minimalism—the core concepts of Zen.

A Short History of Zen

Zen is a school of Mahāyāna Buddhism. The word Zen comes from the Japanese pronunciation of the Chinese word *chán*, which in turn is derived from the Sanskrit word dhyāna, which can be approximately translated as "meditation" or "meditative state". If you mention Zen to many people in the West (well, at least outside of California), they almost always think about fruits and nuts, and not the breakfast cereal variety. ("What kind of craziness are those pot-smoking, surfing yoga instructors up to now, dude?"). But to a large part of the rest of the world, particularly in Asia, Zen is a way of life: a simple, non-materialistic, human-centric existence.

The emergence of Zen as a distinct school of Buddhism was first documented in China in the 7th century CE. From China, Zen spread south to Vietnam, and east to Korea and Japan. As a matter of tradition, the establishment of Zen is credited to the South Indian Pallava prince-turned-monk, Bodhidharma, who came to China during the rise of Tamil Buddhism in Tamilakam to teach a "special transmission outside scriptures, not founded on words or letters."

Thus, Zen developed as a way to concentrate on direct experience rather than on rational creeds or revealed scriptures. Wisdom was passed, not through words or concepts, but through a lineage of one-to-one direct transmission of experience from

39

teacher to student. It is commonly taught that such lineage continued all the way from the Buddha's time to the present.

Although it is difficult to trace when the West first became aware of Zen as a distinct form of Buddhism, the visit of Soyen Shaku, a Japanese Zen monk, to Chicago during the World Parliament of Religions in 1893 is often pointed to as an event that enhanced its profile in the Western world. It was during the late 1950s and the early 1960s that the number of Westerners, other than the descendants of Asian immigrants, pursuing a serious interest in Zen reached a significant level. The first Chinese master to teach Westerners in North America was Hsuan Hua, who taught Chán and other traditions of Chinese Buddhism in San Francisco during the early 1960s.

Although it is a form of Buddhism, Zen does not have to conflict with other organized religions, and many Jews and Christians practice components of Zen. Even those who subscribe to a higher power find it worthwhile to look inside and truly understand themselves. For example, in 1989, the Vatican released a position paper that supported the use of Zen concepts in Christian prayer. Thomas Merton, a Catholic priest, once said, "Without Buddhism I could not be a Christian."

Core Concepts of Zen

The central concept of Zen is mindfulness—becoming intentionally aware of yourself in the present. You focus on the current moment by eliminating distractions and embracing solitude and stillness, letting go of the future and the past, which are both outside of your control.

By clearing our minds of worries and regrets about the future and the past, we begin to pay attention to the present. We cease to be on automatic pilot. When we do this, we begin to understand the true essence of who we are. We recognize our values, desires, and beliefs. From this understanding, we can influence the present to steer us toward a desired future, always knowing that we cannot control the future and we must continually adjust the present.

Focusing on the present is difficult. If you are doing two things at once, e.g., surfing the Internet while talking on the phone, or cooking dinner while watching television, you aren't being mindful. Multitasking, as we'll discuss later, simply doesn't work. Having an inability to focus and be mindful is one reason why.

Meditation is at the core of Zen, and can be as simple as taking a few minutes to sit quietly, removing both internal and external distractions. Embracing solitude and stillness helps you become mindful, aware of yourself, of your breathing, of the thoughts flying through your head. By actively engaging with the present through meditation you become more calm and relaxed, even when you are not intentionally meditating. Eventually, you will be able to find tranquility, even in a noisy room. Imagine being calm while stuck in traffic or flying through O'Hare the day before Thanksgiving. It can happen!

Another way Zen opens our minds is through the use of koans. Koans are stories or riddles with no clear logical answer—or any specific right answer, for that matter. Here's an example of a popular one: "Looking into a well, a man without shadow is draw-

41

ing water. Why?" Koans can drive us nuts (especially Westerners), but by focusing on such riddles, we become more aware of ourselves and the sometimes counterintuitive aspects of our environment. For example, if we are agitated while waiting in a line at a bank, is it the bank's fault, or is it ours for not allowing enough time? At the present moment, unable to control the past or the future, is there value in being agitated? Remember when I mentioned that Lean is often counterintuitive, using the example that it is more efficient to prepare one complete Christmas letter at a time than to separate the steps? Now you are beginning to sense the nexus.

Although Zen creates focus in the present, it does not preclude having goals for the future. There is nothing wrong with goals as long as they reflect the truth that we have discovered inside ourselves. Most self-help books try to change who we are. Zen wants us to discover who we are, then use that as a platform for growth.

A common symbol in Zen is the *ensō*, a circle created with a single brush stroke that symbolizes minimalism, strength, elegance, and the universe. The circle is generally open, indicating the opportunity for improvement while striving for perfection. Similarly, Lean tells us to work continually on small, incremental improvements. Instead of benchmarking against others, Lean organizations compare themselves to perfection.

42

Simplicity (kanso) is another core principle of Zen. Striving toward simplicity in all aspects of our lives helps make it easier to experience and understand the present—in other words, to be mindful. Simplicity creates balance (*kyosei*) and the ability to embrace austerity (*koko*), so we can appreciate what Tanveer Naseer calls the "white spaces," or open spots on our calendar and in our lives.

Zen is humanistic, compassionate, and communal, while at the same time focused within ourselves. We exist in the present with our friends, relatives, coworkers, and fellow citizens. It teaches us that we do not need to feed our egos or acquire more material goods, allowing us to better help others without comparing ourselves to them. The prevalence of this mindset became very evident during the devastating Japanese earthquake and tsunami in early 2011. There was no looting. It simply didn't exist because people were more concerned about their community than themselves.

Zen and Business

There are numerous books describing how Zen can be applied to business, so I will just give you an overview and avoid the minutiae. Zen helps leaders grow by letting them understand their true nature, in the present. Zen helps organizations grow by enabling them to understand their true values and their present state. It helps integrate those into a long-term strategy with supporting activities that are continually adjusted based on events in the present.

One of the most important ways Zen does this is by encouraging simplicity. Our leadership lives are complex. In a 2010 study of over 1,500 chief executive officers by IBM's Institute for Business Value, the number one challenge they faced was "the rapid escalation of complexity." Over 80% predicted even more complexity in the future. Zen's push for simplicity can free up leaders' time and other resources and help them be more effective. In his oft-circulated treatise titled "Things Leaders Do," GE CEO Jeff Immelt pushes leaders to "Simplify constantly—every leader needs to explain the top three things the organization is working on. If you can't, then you're not leading well."

As organizations become more complex, conventional solutions to problems become less effective, so solutions must be out of the box. Zen teaches us to think in new ways, always considering unconventional ideas instead of dismissing them outright. Solutions created in this fashion are more likely to be competitive disruptors.

Zen brings us back to understanding the value of our people, the value of purpose, the importance of ethics. The human side of business is sometimes sacrificed to create future value, and the seductive power of an external extrinsic reward may become overpowering without some level of reflection and introspection that Zen provides. It grounds a leader in the present and reminds him or her what is really important.

The Nexus of Lean and Zen

You may have already noticed some of the similarities between Lean and Zen from the background information presented, but just in case it is still unclear, let's review some of the key parallels to set the perspective for future discussion.

Both Lean and Zen incorporate the concept of awareness through observation. One of the giants of Lean, Taiichi Ohno, had his engineers go and stand in a small circle on the factory floor, sometimes for as long as a day. The intent was to observe the process and look for opportunities for improvement. The long period of time created an immersive experience and removed external distractions. Similarly, Zen awareness centers on the practice of meditation, sitting silently for sometimes long periods of time, and calming the mind so you can observe the true reality of the present.

The concept of simplicity is also fundamental to both Lean and Zen. With Lean, you are continually working to improve a process by removing waste, taking it to its simplest possible state. With Zen, simplicity helps create harmony.

Harmony in Zen is itself akin to the Lean concept of flow. Harmony is balance, effortless flow, and is often described in Zen as like water. Similarly, Ohno also used the water metaphor to describe optimum flow in a factory.

Awareness, simplicity, harmony, balance, and flow. As we'll soon see, these are just the start of the nexus between Lean and Zen.

45

Part Two - Reconnect

Men go abroad to wonder at the heights of mountains, at the huge waves of the sea, at the long courses of the rivers, at the vast compass of the ocean, at the circular motions of the stars, and they pass by themselves without wondering. – Saint Augustine

Before you start to lead, you first need to learn about yourself. The emphasis, at least initially, should be on you. As you read, consider how the concepts in this section can be applied to yourself first, and later transferred to your team and your organization.

Key points from this section:
- Effective organizational leaders first need to effectively lead themselves. This requires reconnecting with who they are.
- Being physically healthy and spiritually connected creates a foundation for improvement and balance.
- Learn about yourself by embracing stillness, quietude, and solitude, and by intentionally breaking your routine.
- Mindful meditation is one of the most powerful (and easiest) methods to calm the mind and be more grounded in the present.

Healthy Body

Physical fitness is the basis for all other forms of excellence.
– John F. Kennedy

Growing up, I was a pretty healthy kid. My parents did a great job of feeding me well. They never let me eat too much junk food, soda, or candy. We stayed active, too. During high school, I was on the swim team, and our family did a LOT of walking while exploring South America, where we lived for seven years.

Then came college, where I discovered beer and pizza. I still remember the look on Mom's face when I came home after that first semester, appearing somewhat rounder than when I left a few months earlier. Maintaining an acceptable weight and over-all good level of fitness became a struggle for the next thirty years, when I was frequently twenty to thirty pounds above my optimum weight.

During that time, being overweight impacted my personal and professional leadership. It hurt my self-confidence, lowered my energy level, and complicated my life. Clothes didn't fit right, so business travel and presentations took more planning.

I would try diets from time to time, but they were not well-planned and lacking in key nutrients, so the weight came back soon after I reached my goal. When I married my vegetarian wife, I became a "pescatarian" (including fish in a vegetarian diet), but, unfortunately, mushroom pizza is also vegetarian, so it was not easy to keep weight off. The best thing I did was to exercise regularly, especially during the last five or ten years. I even ran

48

a full marathon to check one goal off my bucket list, but instead of taking advantage of the training to lose weight, I relished the fact that I could eat a whole pizza at night without gaining more weight! During times of extreme stress, even the exercise went out the window, further aggravating my weight problem.

Then, my friend Paul Akers, a Lean leader about my age who I respect on many levels, told me about his own physical transformation that included losing 50 pounds. He has since written a book about the process called Lean Health. As the title implies, Paul applied Lean concepts to his health. At the most fundamental level, he writes, your body is your customer, and having too much weight and consuming too much food is waste. He created accountability by using a fitness app and by sharing photos of what he was eating, a technique he calls the "photo diet," and he standardized his routine by creating standard foods, exercise, and eating schedules.

With Paul's encouragement, I began applying those same principles, and soon discovered that just about everything I thought I knew about nutrition and portion size was wrong. I adjusted portion sizes, eliminated unnecessary carbohydrates such as bread at dinner, and worked to balance my nutritional intake. In six months, I dropped thirty pounds while also meeting my balanced nutritional needs. The new diet, combined with the strength and aerobic conditioning I had been focusing on for the previous couple years, made me fitter than I have been since before college, more than thirty years ago. I feel great, and am more mentally sharp. Since I was careful to create a diet and exercise routine that I could be comfortable with over the long term, I have been able to sustain the improvements.

Good sleeping habits have also helped me improve my health. Without good rest, exercise and proper nutrition are much less effective. Most experts recommend eight or even nine hours of sleep each night, but that can vary considerably. In my case, a little over six hours, coincidentally about two REM cycles, seems best. Unless I have an important meeting or flight, I never set my alarm and still wake up around four. I don't drink caffeinated coffee, but feel very alert until noon. I'll often take a quick thirty-minute nap right after lunch, leaving me invigorated for the rest of the day. Figure out what amount of sleep works for you, erring on the longer side, and keeping in mind that experts probably recommend more than you think you need. Getting enough rest will multiply the effects of exercise and proper nutrition.

A fit body creates the foundation for a fit mind. Treat your body as your most important customer, reduce waste, gain energy, and create balance and harmony in your mind. This will help you be a more effective leader.

Connected Spirit

We are not human beings on a spiritual journey.
We are spiritual beings on a human journey.
– Stephen R. Covey

The majority of humans believe in some type of a connection to a greater power, be it truly divine or just universal. Some may believe but simply go through motions drilled into them since birth, never questioning or validating the experience. Some, like myself, affirm the existence of something else—even if we don't understand what that is.

The scientist in me stares up at the stars, knowing there are countless billions of them potentially with civilizations vastly older and more developed than ours. Then I contemplate recent advances in fields like quantum mechanics, where entanglement creates instantaneous connections over vast distances, making me wonder if we're starting to see the connection between the physical world and the soul. I see how the evolution of the "internet of things" has already made billions of devices instantly accessible and controllable, and wonder how long will it be before every molecule in our world can be similarly addressed and manipulated.

The curious learner in me has spent years reading and analyzing numerous books on the history of religions, and I am amazed at the remarkable similarities between them. As one religious scholar friend once told me, it's as if different groups of people were watching the same game from different parts of a stadium—some from the front row, others from high up in the standing-room-only section, still others from behind obstructions where they could only see part of the field. Each group recorded their experience in ways that were then distorted over time.

Episcopalian bishop and theologian John Shelby Spong has written about the impact of perspectives on religious literalism. One example he gives is the many ways ancient peoples described the rise of the sun each morning, from it being a star to being the powerful god Ra. Culture, religion, and knowledge shaped how different groups understood the same event. Other theologians,

51

such as Catholic priest Thomas Merton, have found how seem-ingly disparate religions, such as Buddhism and Christianity, can be very complementary.

Like many people, I have felt an unequivocal, undeniable force at many times in my life. When dealing with exceptional stress, loss, or difficult decisions, it was there. It's no longer faith for me—it's real. I feel it while walking in nature, or even at this very moment, while looking out over the Caribbean while on vacation.

Each person's experience is unique. But take time, perhaps while surrounded by the beauty of nature, to contemplate your spiritual existence. Being able to draw strength from that will bring peace. Peace will help calm your mind, enabling you to understand who you are.

Forgive Yourself

Forgive yourself. It sounds simple, but don't think for a second that it is easy. Getting free from the tyranny of past mistakes can be hard work, but definitely worth the effort. And the payoff is health, wholeness and inner peace. In other words, you get your life back.
– Steve Goodier

We've all messed up, even folks like Mother Teresa and Mahatma Gandhi made mistakes. So why do screw-ups burden us so much? The burden can sometimes overwhelm us, change our perspective, create excess caution, and severely impact our leader-ship effectiveness.

Like everyone, I've had some doozies. Some are simply

humorous or embarrassing, some I'm ashamed of, and some still make me cringe knowing how close I came to radically changing my life. Fortunately, I've always been able to move on fairly easily, sometimes perhaps too much so. As just one small example, nearly twenty years ago, I was hurrying through a store when I came up to an elderly woman blocking a narrow aisle. I moved around her a little too quickly and carelessly, nearly causing her to fall. I immediately felt remorse. To this day, I vividly remember the look on her face and on the faces of others around me, as well as how ashamed I felt. It was a mistake, but I couldn't change it. I had to forgive myself and learn from the experience.

The past is the past. Nothing is going to change it. To be at peace, you must accept that you will make mistakes. Learn from them, remember them just enough so that you know not to repeat it, make amends if appropriate, and move on. If you knew of someone else that had your past, how would you treat them? Probably with compassion. Do the same to yourself.

Gratitude

Be thankful for what you have; you'll end up having more.
If you concentrate on what you don't have,
you will never, ever have enough.
– Oprah Winfrey

Oftentimes we become so focused on fixing problems and resolving issues that our entire sense of reality shifts. We begin to live in a bubble that encompasses the negative and blocks the positive. Because they demand our attention, the negative aspects of work and life consume a disproportionate amount of our thinking, and eventually distorts our perceived reality.

You can re-center your perspective by grounding yourself in thanks for what is good with you or your team. What are you thankful for? Think about your health, your relationships, your business success. There will be more to be thankful for than you realize. Use a few minutes in the shower each morning, the first few minutes of your meditation, or even the first few minutes of each staff meeting to identify specific people and situations to be thankful for. Try to say thanks to at least one person each day, meaningfully and mindfully. Even better, write someone a thank-you note by hand. Make it a self-sustaining habit, a routine.

I have much to be thankful for: my parents teaching me the joy of learning, which eventually led me to discover Lean and Zen; my wife teaching me how to be more compassionate, which has completely changed my perspective on life; and business partners and associates that have put up with some of my wild ideas.

Reflecting on gratitude at the beginning and end of each day creates calm bookends to what can be chaos for me. As problem solvers, we are naturally predisposed to focus on the negative, taking for granted the positive to the extent that we often become oblivious and unaware of just how much positive there is in our lives. Intentionally focusing on gratitude brings that perspective back to reality. Expressing gratitude in daily life, complimenting and helping others, or just smiling, reinforces the power of being thankful. Intentionally finding gratitude every day, has changed my perspective on life more than any other personal or professional leadership habit. I've discovered I have a lot to be thankful for, which helps me be more generous, sympathetic, and empathetic.

Self-Inquiry

On a deeper level you are already complete. When you realize that, there is a joyous energy behind what you do.
– Eckhart Tolle

Last year, some colleagues and I were discussing books we've found to be interesting, and my business partner suggested Edgar Schein's *Humble Inquiry: The Gentle Art of Asking Instead of Telling*. I read the book and loved it.

Schein describes three types of humility and four types of inquiry, focusing on the power of here-and-now humility. This form of humility happens when we presume to be dependent on someone else because that someone has something we need (e.g., knowledge). Consider the following excerpt:

> What we ask, how we ask it, where we ask it, and when we ask it all matter. But the essence of Humble Inquiry goes beyond just overt questioning. The kind of inquiry I am talking about derives from an attitude of interest and curiosity. It implies a desire to build a relationship that will lead to more open communication. It also implies that one makes oneself vulnerable and, thereby, arouses positive helping behavior in the other person.

It strikes me that, although Schein was intending to describe a relationship between two or more people, his concepts are also very appropriate for our discussions with ourselves (assuming we have them). Creating a humble, vulnerable relationship with yourself opens you up to being able to inquire, discover, reflect, and perhaps create change. Accepting yourself for who you are gives you peace. We'll discuss reflection in more detail later on.

Seek Stillness and Quietude

I will take time to be quiet. In this silence I will listen...
and I will hear my answers.
– Ruth Fishel

We live chaotic lives, often surrounded by noise and commotion. We deal with kids, coworkers, traffic, and the barrage of thoughts in our own minds. We move constantly, almost as a way to show that we're active and productive.

What would happen if you just sat and listened? If, in the middle of the chaos, you were simply quiet and still? How would you, your team (or family) react? How would it impact your perception (and reality) of strength, wisdom, and confidence? How would it help you to understand yourself and help others to grow?

There is a power that comes from stillness and quietude. Pausing actually adds information and context to our lives. Being quiet calms us, and then calms others. A quiet leadership style provides the time to observe, contemplate, connect, and focus, both on the world around us and within on our own thoughts.

My wife and I try to make time for being quiet. When we are together, we regularly discuss the activities of our day and upcoming decisions we need to make. But we'll also sit on a beach or enjoy breakfast on the porch together, observing the world in silence. The silence actually creates an emotional bond between us, strengthened by quietly sharing the nature around us.

Be still, be quiet, and observe what is happening around you.

Embrace Solitude

Solitude gives birth to the original in us,
to beauty, unfamiliar and perilous....
– Thomas Mann

We have become used to a world that floods our senses and keeps us entertained 24/7. Think back to a time before radio and TV, perhaps even before books. Besides working to increase the population, what did people do? They thought, and pondered, and created new ideas. They learned about others and themselves. In the modern world, we've lost some of that ability, and we need to make a conscious effort to get it back.

When we're alone, with just ourselves and when not overtly meditating, our thoughts gel and reassemble into priorities and actionable concepts. What used to be a jumble begins to make sense. Conflicting priorities give way to clear direction. Seemingly insurmountable obstacles are put in their proper perspective. Most of us have experienced this, either alone or perhaps when our team is at an offsite meeting (in solitude as a team).

As I described in the introduction, the power of solitude was my first experience with Zen. In the midst of personal and professional chaos, I flew myself to Hawaii on a few hours notice, and just sat on a beach. I breathed in the fragrant air, listened to the birds and waves, and had a glass of wine by myself. My thoughts slowed, my priorities realigned, and I reconnected with myself.

Lately, I've found I can obtain the same benefit by driving with the radio off, taking a walk on the nearby beach, or even just sitting on the porch in the morning. Alone, just my thoughts and me.

Embrace solitude as an intentional part of your leadership routine. Take your daily commute with the radio turned off, or go for a weekly walk on an empty beach. Find a place to be alone, even if it is just a few times a year while on vacation (many executives plan a couple days alone at the end of business trips). The more frequently you make solitude part of your leadership habits, the more settled and aligned your thoughts will be. In addition to having it be part of your personal routine, consider ways to make solitude a part of your team's dynamics, such as via offsite meetings.

Break the Routine

New habits can be powerful. But habits can also create barriers that limit our perspective, which can hinder kaizen, creativity, and even our knowledge of ourselves. This is known as the proverbial "rut," and we've all been there at times in our lives.

Sometimes you just need a break to re-center, recalibrate, recharge, or readjust your horizons. In the Zen world, this is *datsuzoku*, a break from the routine. Datsuzoku can be as simple as getting a good night's sleep or as common as taking a week of vacation.

I try to insert breaks in my routines in many ways. My wife and I visit a couple of new countries each year—we're up to over sixty now. Later on, I'll tell you about how every year for over twenty years I've had an annual goal to do or learn something different. These have included running a marathon, learning HTML programming, and researching Biblical history. Each month, I try to read a book on a topic I otherwise wouldn't have been interested in. Each week, I take some time for myself and try to find a new place to walk. With all of these breaks, my perspectives change and I learn something.

What habits or activities do you have at home, at work, or with your team, that need to be examined? What would happen if you broke those routines? What would you learn? How would perspectives change? Could it enable change or innovation?

Be Present, Aware, and Mindful

If we are not fully ourselves, truly in the present moment,
we miss everything.
– Thich Nhat Hanh

Many people have a problem with letting go of the past, no matter if it is painful or pleasant. Not me, however. I've always been able to let go of the past almost immediately. My problem has been letting go of the future.

Ever since my first job, I've been a planner. I've been able to see and develop pathways to future goals, and in most cases that has served me well. Over time, especially as my professional responsibilities increased, the level and detail of the planning increased. When I was faced with the chaotic family medical situation for a few years, my level of planning reached obsessive levels. I would literally have future plans laid out in excruciating detail, with contingency plans A, B, C and D for each potential obstacle. I spent hours every day thinking about plans, tweaking strategies and tactics, both personally and professionally. I spent hours identifying potential corrective actions to situations that, if even the worst occurred, might take a few minutes to fix—if they were even worth fixing.

I blame this obsession with planning on my first boss, who told me to "sweat the details." That simple statement apparently triggered some OCD-inducing neurochemical pathway in my brain. But before you tell me that I need to check myself in to a rehab facility, let me tell you that I've changed.

60

The change began a few years ago (surprisingly, without professional intervention) by the Lean guy in me realizing it was ridiculous to spend more time planning contingencies than it would take to simply deal with problems that might not occur. This was a waste, and it was a struggle to overcome. I had to be okay with problems arising. I soon learned that, as the cliché states, problems are opportunities to learn.

The change in my mindset was fortified by the realization that I was missing what was happening in the present by focusing so much on the future. Time had flown by and I hadn't even noticed. I had experienced many great things, but I didn't remember them. I remember one day when I was standing in the middle of our production floor, trying to channel Taiichi Ohno and simply observe the process. After nearly an hour, I realized I had spent the previous fifty-five minutes thinking about solutions to a problem I had noticed in the first five minutes on the floor. I completely missed the fact that the production team had also seen the problem and had already resolved it. What a space case! I needed to work on focus, on being present.

The emphasis on being mindful of the present moment is perhaps Zen's most distinctive characteristic. In our western relationship with time, we compulsively pick over the past in order to learn lessons from it, and then project into a hypothetical future how those lessons can be applied. The present moment has been compressed to a tiny sliver on the clock face between a vast past and an infinite future. Zen, more than anything else, is about reclaiming and expanding the present moment.

There are many exercises that can help us become more

present. By turning off the radio in the car, deliberately trying to experience each of the five senses while walking, or spending time alone in silence, you can slowly learn to be more aware of the present. Feel the warmth of the sun, the chill of the wind, the sound of the crickets, and the conversations of people around you. Practice during routine activities such as brushing your teeth, and especially when you are having to wait.

Being mindful is being truly aware of your surroundings and what you are doing. Why are you doing what you're doing? What is the purpose? Who is the customer? What is the expected result? Does it create value? Is there a better way of doing it?

It's important to be aware that mindfulness can be uncomfortable, especially in the beginning. You will notice and confront difficult feelings and thoughts, but recognizing and coming to terms with them is critical for self-awareness.

Focus on purposely and deliberately being in the present. Listen to what your spouse or team members are saying, without thinking about last night's football game or tomorrow's presentation. Watch the sunset without wondering what's for dinner. When you have a couple of spare minutes between meetings or when you first come into the office, don't check your phone or strike up a conversation. Just sit and observe the present.

Just Chill

In a controversy, the instant we feel anger, we have already ceased striving for the truth, and have begun striving for ourselves.
– Buddha

We all get angry from time to time. A task isn't completed as we would have expected, a situation seems insurmountable, and the tension builds. Perhaps a key customer, or even your spouse, is angry.

When this happens, be wary of blowing things out of proportion. Very few decisions, actions, or issues are truly catastrophic. Don't elevate them to that level through your own response. Ask yourself why it feels so important, and if that is valid. Be mindful and realistic about the worst-case outcome. Think about what the situation will look like in hindsight a year from now. Will you even remember it? Can it be turned into a positive mentoring or learning opportunity for you, your team, or your family?

Count to ten. Just chill.

Meditate

You should sit in meditation for twenty minutes a day,
unless you are too busy;
then you should sit for an hour.
– Old Zen Saying

Meditation is a practice that teaches you to be mindful of the world around you, mindful of your body and soul, and mindful of the present moment. Being aware of the world around you, and especially your own mind, is surprisingly difficult. Like waste in a Lean environment, the majority of the thoughts in your head are repetitive and not useful, and the noise can drown out real insight. But once you become more aware of your thoughts and the patterns of those thoughts, you will be able to exert more control over yourself. Meditation is the act, mindfulness is the state it creates.

By focusing inward, you become aware of your self-doubt, self-criticism, and rationalization. Over time, you learn to recognize whether those thoughts are valid. This is why methods to focus inward, including meditation, are used extensively by mental health professionals. Meditation can even cause a physiological response, with some research showing that it leads to a reduction in age-related brain deterioration. A 2012 Harvard study in *Frontiers of Human Neuroscience* showed that "meditation can improve emotional stability and response to stress." A 2011 Yale study in *Proceedings of the National Academy of Science* showed that "experienced meditators seem to switch off areas of the brain associated with wandering thoughts, anxiety, and some psychiatric disorders such as schizophrenia."

As Shawn Achor and Michelle Gielan described in a recent Harvard Business Review article, many companies, including Google, Aetna, General Mills, Intel, and Target, recognize the power of mindful meditation to reduce stress, deprogram multitasking tendencies, and improve focus. After practicing meditation for a month, a group of Intel employees reported a twenty percent decrease in stress, a thirty percent increase in overall happiness and well-being, and a twenty percent increase in new ideas, the ability to focus, and the quality of work relationships.

To start a meditation practice, pick a time of the day when you will not be disturbed or distracted. I personally prefer to meditate right after I get up, before breakfast and definitely before I check email or read the paper. (If you put it off, you will never get to it—trust me.) Some people find it beneficial to engage in brief exercise or yoga to release energy so the mind is better prepared for meditation. (In fact, this purpose was one of the of origins of yoga.)

Find a quiet location with few distractions—for me, it is a corner of my downstairs office. Traditional meditation starts by sitting cross-legged on a *zafu* (small cushion) but this is not a requirement. Whether you sit on a chair or a cushion, it is important to be upright with your body balanced. I prefer to face the wall to further reduce distractions, and I use a timer app on my iPad so I won't be distracted by wanting to check the clock.

Rest your hands in your lap and look downward, with your eyes opened and focused downward a few feet away. Keeping your eyes open helps you remain present, but if you need to initially close your eyes to remove distractions, go ahead. Focusing on an object, such as a candle or a tree out the window, can also help remove distractions. Take a slow, deep breath and feel it enter, then exit, the lungs. Count each breath.

Acknowledge and accept the thoughts that will inevitably enter your head, then cast them aside by refocusing on your breathing. You will be surprised at how difficult it is to even count to ten without having an extraneous thought. After a little practice, you will learn to enjoy the simple breathing, the serenity it creates, and the joy of realizing that breathing means you are alive.

Initially, do this for just two or three minutes, eventually working up to ten or fifteen. When you find you can regularly count ten breaths without distraction, stop counting and just count in, out, in, out, 1, 2, 1, 2. Otherwise you will get too caught up in the counting itself.

After a week or a month, if you are comfortably counting breaths, add some concentration to the practice. As you breathe in, consciously follow the breath from your mouth to the depths of your lungs, and then do the reverse as you exhale. Take several seconds to inhale and exhale, deliberately being conscious and aware of how the air feels. Feel the breath oxygenate your blood, notice how your heartbeat changes, feel the breath take the turn at the top of your throat. As before, if your mind wanders, recognize the thoughts, dispatch them, and return your focus to your breath.

Once you can effortlessly count breaths and focus on how breathing changes your body for twenty or thirty minutes, the next step is to add whole-body awareness. As you breathe in and out, focus on the top of your body and work your way down, following the breath. Be aware of each itch and each pain, and identify their exact location. What do you feel when you mentally explore the itch instead of scratching? When you reach the tips of your toes, work your way back up. Over time you'll be amazed at how you can feel sensations you never felt before, how itches can move, and how you begin to recognize the wonder that is your body. You will also learn how you can remove muscle tension and stress just by recognizing it.

When I began to include whole-body awareness in my meditation, it took me well over a month to work up to just fifteen minutes. As you reach that point, you will notice a significant improvement in serenity and calmness, which will help reinforce your practice by offsetting the effort it initially takes. My current daily meditation is twenty-five minutes. If I'm stressed, I force myself to meditate for an hour, although I still cannot keep my mind clear for that length of time.

A couple times a week I will also do *kinhin*, or walking meditation, on the beach near our house. Although kinhin is technically used as a walking break between periods of sitting meditation, I find it to be a break from my daily routine and a powerful bonding time with nature. Walk-ing meditation is very similar to sitting meditation except that you take one step per breath, still focusing on your breathing, thoughts, and body. I also enjoy doing it barefoot to add additional sensory inputs and a closer sense of connection to the Earth.

Walking, unfortunately, is often looked down on in the West. Even the term "pedestrian" is often used as a synonym for "limited in scope." However, walking—especially purposeless walking—can stimulate creativity. Some of history's greats, such as C.S. Lewis, Charles Dickens, George Orwell, Friedrich Nietzsche, Virginia Wolfe, and Henry David Thoreau have been stimulated by walking. The key is to walk, free of distractions, with no audiobooks, music, or even companions. Just you and the world around you.

Meditation is the easiest way to calm the mind and become more in touch with the present reality. Try it for a few days and take note of how you feel, of how your thoughts change. You will notice yourself becoming more perceptive, calm, and present in personal and professional situations. This is why many organizations, sports teams, and health professionals are encouraging their team members to meditate. The benefits of meditation far outweigh the cost of the time it takes to perform it.

(Note: Though it is an important part of Zen, meditation is not in itself religious. It is neither prayer nor contemplation. However, it can augment those activities when combined with them. For more tips on how to meditate, visit the online resources section at the back of this book.)

Part Three – Create

You cannot eat every tadpole and frog in the pond,
but you can eat the biggest and ugliest one,
and that will be enough, at least for the time being.
– Brian Tracy

By now we've explored how to reconnect and understand ourselves. Before we dive into the work of clarifying, planning, and improving, we'd better figure out how to be more productive.

Key points from this section:
- Distractions are productivity killers, and need to be minimized. Multitasking is a form of distraction.
- Learn your most productive periods of the day, protect them, and use them to your advantage.
- Journaling lets you download your brain, track issues and projects, and reflect on performance. This produces learning.
- Create an intentional routine that makes higher productivity a habit.

Remove Distractions

You will never reach your destination
if you stop and throw stones at every dog that barks.
– Winston S. Churchill

When many people go into the office, they start their day by chatting with some colleagues, checking their email, and surfing the net for a while. Then they start working on whatever project is due that day. Soon, however, they hear the sound of a new email arriving, which they promptly open, leading them to other tasks. Before they know it, the day is over and they still don't have that project finished. This happens repeatedly, making a thirty-minute task take two days to complete.

Every interruption requires time to refocus, and during that interval we lose momentum, either physical or mental. We may be very disciplined with what tasks we want to accomplish and in what order, but we can still fail at actually getting them done.

In most cases, distractions are self-inflicted: choosing to answer an email that could wait, saying hello to everyone that walks by, multitasking, or trying to find the end of the Internet. If you want to be more productive, it helps to get rid of the distractions that demand your attention. This could require you to communicate and manage expectations at your workplace. For example, you might need to explain to colleagues why you are keeping your door shut or not answering emails for a certain time period each morning.

I get easily distracted by physical things—pictures, books,

70

knickknacks, scraps of paper, and the like. Therefore, I work very hard to have a clean, organized work area. Several times a week, I straighten it up, transferring notes to my journal (you might wonder why didn't they go in there in the first place—me too), emptying the trash, scanning and shredding paperwork, and cleaning up my computer desktop. I'm working on trying to standardize this activity, but it's hard.

Another way to be more productive is to understand how you work best. Everyone has an optimum length of time that they can focus on something. For most people, this is between twenty and ninety minutes, after which their attention spans rapidly decrease. For me, that amount of time is about one hour, after which a speck of dust is intriguing enough to divert my attention.

Figure out what the best time interval is for you and leverage it. I use a timer application on my computer (and one on my iPhone when I'm away from the office). I set it for fifty minutes, giving me a ten-minute break every hour. All potential distractions, such as email, web browsers, and even my phone are turned off. (This type of focused work/break sequence is commonly called a *pomodoro*. Francesco Cirillo coined the term in his book, *The Pomodoro Technique*. Pomodoro, which means "tomato" in Italian, refers to the tomato-shaped kitchen timer Cirillo uses to divide his work time in to focused, manageable intervals.)

Once I start my timer, I'll then work on one task for those fifty minutes, stopping for a ten-minute break at the end. During my break time, I try not to check my email, as email seems to draw me in for far longer than ten minutes. (In fact, I'm working at trying to check email just two or three times a day.) When the

71

break is over, I start another fifty minutes. I repeat this cycle as many times as I can, especially during my most productive time of the day.

Years ago, the concept of multitasking was all the rage, and the "ability" to multitask was seen as a positive skill. Thankfully, that's changing, because multitasking is really an effective way to amplify distractions. In *A Factory of One*, Daniel Markovitz describes how multitasking also increases the likelihood of errors and poor quality. One of the key Lean concepts is one-piece flow, i.e., working on one part at a time. The same applies to personal productivity. Focus on just one task at a time instead of many, and you will significantly raise your productivity.

The Big Three

Things which matter most
must never be at the mercy of things which matter least.
– Johann Wolfgang von Goethe

Like most people, I maintain a fairly long to-do list of personal and professional projects. It's a few pages long—especially the honey-do portion. Because the list can be intimidating, I need a good strategy to tackle it. Going about it sequentially isn't appropriate, since the tasks have varying levels of importance and time sensitivity, so each morning, I take a few moments to review my list and decide on the "Big Three" tasks that I want to get accomplished that day. Just three—no more, no less. Sometimes, one of the three may only take ten minutes, but if it rises to the importance of being one of the top three, then it deserves a spot. Maybe I'll have time to work on a fourth task during the day, but I won't include it on the list. By limiting the number to just three, you are forced to prioritize and focus on getting the best return in the short period of just one day.

The Big Three become the focus for the day, and I list them in my journal to ensure I stay on track. I try very hard not to insert another priority that may arise during the day, unless it absolutely, positively has to be there. (If such grenades are being launched into your schedule on a regular basis, then you might have other organizational or process issues to deal with.)

At the end of the day, I reflect on the day's activities, including the Big Three. If I did not finish one of them, I try to understand what happened and what barriers I encountered. Did I underestimate the scope of a task? Was I distracted or interrupted? Did a different high priority task "grenade" get lobbed into my day? If so, why? Was it truly more important, or just more interesting? After figure out the barriers, I try to put countermeasures into place to do better next time. Through this process, I've learned a lot about myself.

I've used this Big Three method for nearly ten years and although it is simple, it has probably created the largest boost in my productivity out of anything I have tried. It is amazing how much you can get done over a week, month, or year if you just finish three key tasks every day.

The Hour of Power

O great creator of being grant us one more hour to perform
our art and perfect our lives.
– Jim Morrison

When you think about your days, including the weekends, do you see a pattern of times when you're most productive? Studies have shown that there is an hour or so each day when we're especially focused and energetic. For many of us, the time is early in the morning (perhaps a relic of our caveman past, when we had to get out early to find food for the family). For others, productivity spikes at other times of the day. Friends and colleagues have told me that their best times to work are mid-morning, afternoon, or even late in the evening.

Over the years, I've found that my most productive time, my "Hour of Power," is from five to six in the morning. Realizing that particular hour is my most productive, I protect it at all cost and schedule nothing during that time, except for the first and most important (and usually most difficult) of my daily Big Three tasks. I take care of other morning activities such as eating, reading the paper, going to the gym, and meditation, before five a.m. Otherwise, they get delayed until afterwards. I also prepare to work on the task before my Hour of Power begins so that I don't sacrifice any of that valuable time trying to figure out where to start.

During the hour, I remove all distractions and focus solely on the task at hand. At the end of it, I mindfully make a decision on whether to continue. I often discover that I have finished the task.

Either that, or I am exhausted and need a break before continuing.

Experiment and discover when your Hour of Power is. Then protect it and take advantage of that period of heightened clarity and focus to give a kick to your productivity.

Leverage Productive Time

Amateurs sit and wait for inspiration,
he rest of us just get up and go to work.
– Stephen King

Similar to the Hour of Power is the concept that certain parts of the day are more productive than others. Once again we're all different in this respect, and it's why some people are "morning people" while others prefer the evenings. I once even had a star employee who worked best from one to three in the morning, and insisted on being in the office at that time. (I won't divert our discussion by describing the other problems that caused.)

I've long known that the most productive time of my day is in the mornings, especially the early mornings. I almost never set an alarm, but am generally awake at four. I take care of my morning meditation, breakfast, reading the paper, and then start the Hour of Power. After the Hour of Power, I usually hit the gym for an hour of strength or cardio work. After a quick shower, I head to the office, attend our morning team video call (our version of the "standup meeting" meeting I'll describe later), and then get back into my productive time. I'll use the pomodoro method to optimize the use of that time, which lasts until 11:30 a.m. or so.

75

While I find that my mornings are usually very productive, afternoons are far more difficult. I find it harder to maintain focus, even when removing distractions, and I know my mental acuity is not at the level it was in the morning. Therefore, I schedule phone calls, more mindless tasks, and errands during this time. A couple times a week, I'll also take do a walking meditation on the beach. During this time, work (improvement) is still being done, just not the most critical tasks. I'm working on improving my mental productivity in the afternoon, but so far nothing has changed—perhaps reinforcing how powerful the productive time of my day is.

Evenings are a bit better than the afternoons, but my priority in the evening is my family. Therefore, I purposely don't schedule any work tasks during this part of the day. When I have evening free time—which is common, since my wife requires more sleep than I do—I use the evenings to catch up on reading. If my brain feels a bit fried, I'll turn on the TV. I end the evening with some reflection.

Deal with it Now

He who waits to do a great deal of good at once
will never do anything.
- Samuel Johnson

So how many questions, issues, and decisions are bouncing around in your head? As an elderly family member aged I became increasingly frustrated with how she was making her life complex when it didn't need to be. Simple decisions, eventually even tasks such as deciding what to watch on TV, became impossible. Her anxiety was skyrocketing and I realized it was a vicious cycle.

The more we put off decisions and tasks, the more we are juggling in our heads. This makes it increasingly difficult to calmly and rationally evaluate an issue and come to a conclusion, which just adds to the chaos.

Stop the cycle. Do you really need more time or more data to evaluate an issue? Sometimes you legitimately do in order to stay focused on a task at hand, but I bet you'd be surprised how often you don't. Think about what more information you'd really need and whether it would change your mind. What is the worst that could happen if you were wrong?

Take the extra second and make the decision. When an employee asks to talk to you, do it now rather than putting it off. Deal with it once, then it is out of your head, decluttering your mind.

Journal

The discipline of writing something down
is the first step toward making it happen.
– Lee Iacocca

As you become more mindful of yourself and your world and formally reflect on the gaps between what you want to happen and what really happens, you will have a lot of "Ah ha!" realizations. Some will stay in your head, but most won't, especially as you get older. This is why you should keep a journal.

77

In his book, *Getting Things Done*, David Allen discusses how the brain is made for processing information, not storing it. As I age, I become more and more aware of how true this is. In fact, I'd say that my processing capabilities have actually improved, while my storage, or at least the speed of accessing that storage, has declined a bit.

Because of this, I try to record or write down as many of my thoughts as possible, as soon as possible. Whenever I have an idea, a new task or project, a new meeting, or someone to call, I immediately jot it down in my journal. In effect, I am downloading my brain. A key, therefore, is that the journal needs to be with you everywhere. We've all had those great ideas during the day without anything nearby to record them.

Keeping a journal will ensure you capture those brilliant sparks of wisdom. When you write your journal, you should record your plans, the results of carrying out those plans, the factors causing the gaps between your expectations and your results, and any insights from your reflec-
tions. This same process can be applied to team meetings, family meet-ings, and mentoring or counseling sessions with individuals. As part of  your reflections, consider past experiences and insights that have been documented in your journal. Do patterns emerge? How do those patterns change your awareness? What will you do about it?

There are many different technologies that can be used

to keep a journal. Electronic journals have become the rage, and I've tried many devices and apps, but they just don't work for me. Instead, I prefer paper notebooks. Instead of having to open my iPad, turn it on, select the right app, and then start writing in a clumsy manner, I just open my Moleskine and start scribbling with a pen or pencil. I start a new journal each year, beginning with an annual end-of-year reflection where I look back at the past year and think about personal and professional goals for the upcoming one. I'll tell you more about that reflection process later on.

Each morning before I start work, I write down my Big Three tasks for the day and I take a moment to record something I'm grateful for. It's amazing how that creates focus and a positive perspective. During the day, I sketch out ideas and keep a list of to-do's. And at the end of the day, I review and reflect (*hansei*) on my Big Three and on the rest of my day to see if I accomplished what I set out to do. If I didn't, I write down how to improve next time. I also jot down action items, notes from phone calls, and questions to follow up on. Roughly once a week, I review previous pages, putting a check mark in the top corner of each page that no longer has open items (an easily seen visual cue). Every month or so, I do a more thorough review, copying uncompleted action items and issues to a new page so I don't have to skim through the journal to find them.

All this seems cumbersome, right? Could this be done more effectively electronically? Probably for some people, but not for me. Writing by hand is powerful for me. Experiment and discover what works best for you. The important action is the recording and reviewing, however it is done.

Kanban Work

These days, thanks to a simplified personal and professional life, my task list isn't very complex. It's lengthy, but not convoluted; therefore, a simple list in my journal works very well. However, this was not always the case, and probably isn't the case for many of you. To simplify your task list, one tool you can use is a kanban.

Kanban, meaning "signal" or "card" in Japanese, is a way to define and visually show the work, and components of work, in a sequence of operations. Kanban boards for personal or knowl-edge work were developed by the agile software development community and inspired by how Toyota manages work-in-process. The boards have a series of columns,

with the leftmost one being the parking lot or backlog, holding tasks that are waiting to start. The next column to the right is for tasks that are ready to start, labeled as "Ready" or "This Month." Then comes the "Today" column and, if you really want to tightly manage it, one for "Big Three." Finally, a column for "Done" so you can see (and celebrate!) results. I often used additional columns for tasks that had been delegated, or were waiting on external input.

Although a simple whiteboard works for most people, vari-ous apps and programs exist to use the kanban concept to manage task lists. Be careful to not allow a software solution to overcomplicate a simple process. Magnetic cards, or even sticky notes, can be used for tasks, making it easy to move them around. Additional visual cues can be developed and used to indicate priority and the amount of time estimated to complete the task. I would date the cards so I could easily tell how long were aging—perhaps an indicator in itself of importance.

Kanban is just one potential tool for task management, and there are many potential variations of it. Experiment, don't simply adopt. Figure out what works best for you.

Confront Mortality

There is only one true wealth in all the universe—living time.
– Frank Herbert

I was hesitant about discussing this topic, but decided it truly does impact my perspective on work and life. As we get older (I'm now in my 50s), the end of our lives—our impending doom, rebirth, or whatever you believe—is more on our minds. Whether we like it or not, our mortality can motivate us to be more productive. We each have a finite amount of time in this existence (sadly for some, less than we expect). Make the best use of it. Being aware (mindful) of my mortality has added focus and priority to what I want to get done, both personally and professionally.

Experiencing how time seems to accelerate as I age (and recognizing that there's a finite amount of it), has encouraged me to look at how I'm consuming my limited inventory of minutes.

What projects and activities truly create value from the customer's (my) perspective? What projects, accomplishments, and dreams have I been putting off? Do I have the right balance of professional and personal activities?

I want to be careful to not overdo it, however. Even at my age, I have some friends and family who are still too single-mindedly focused on a career or ambition, even if they do not like it. In your own life, ensure there's balance, explore other aspects of life, do something you enjoy and learn from. There isn't much time left.

The Intentional Routine

Routine, in an intelligent man, is a sign of ambition.
– W. H. Auden

One common characteristic of many successful people is that they fill their days with well-defined routines. These routines, when done intentionally, are what allow people to grow their skills and capabilities to the point where they stand out from others in their particular field.

Last year, I came across a passage in the book *Kurt Vonnegut: Letters*, a fascinating, funny, and—since it's Vonnegut—sometimes freaky book that takes you inside the mind of the famous author. The quote below comes from a letter he wrote to his wife Jane, in which he describes his daily routine:

In an unmoored life like mine, sleep and hunger and work arrange themselves to suit themselves, without consulting me. I'm just as glad they haven't consulted me about the tiresome details. What they have worked out is this: I awake at 5:30, work until 8:00, eat breakfast at home, work until 10:00, walk a few blocks into town, do errands, go to the nearby municipal swimming pool, which I have all to myself, and swim for half an hour, return home at 11:45, read the mail, eat lunch at noon. In the afternoon I do schoolwork, either teach or prepare. When I get home from school at about 5:30, I numb my twanging intellect with several belts of Scotch and water ($5.00/fifth at the State Liquor store, the only liquor store in town. There are loads of bars, though.), cook supper, read and listen to jazz (lots of good music on the radio here), slip off to sleep at ten.

Benjamin Franklin is also famous for his routine, which he meticulously tracked in a daily log. Franklin based his routine on two main questions: At the beginning of the day, he asked himself, *what good shall I do today?* At the end of the day, he asked, *what good have I done today?* In other words, Franklin would decide what he wanted to accomplish for the day first thing in the morning, then in the evening, he would reflect on how successful he had been.

Reflection (along with gratitude, as I previously discussed) is a key attribute of leadership success. Reflection forces you to look back at your processes and results and, most importantly, provides the introspection and analysis to improve your routine and performance. Reflecting at the end of the day turns common habits into an intentional routine. It gives you an awareness of your routines and makes you purposeful about what you do throughout your day.

Every evening, you should look back at your day and ask how your routine affected your performance for the day. You should ask how effective your task selection itself is, as well as how your routine can be improved to better support task completion. Answering these questions converts simple habits into an intentional, high-performing routine, which is unquestionably worth a few minutes of your time each evening.

The morning question, What good shall I do this day?	5	Rise, wash, and address Power-
	6	ful Goodness; contrive day's busi-
	7	ness and take the resolution of the day; prosecute the present
	8	study; and breakfast.
	9	Work.
	10	
	11	
	12	Read or overlook my accounts,
	1	and dine.
	2	
	3	Work.
	4	
	5	
	6	Put things in their places, sup-
	7	per, music, or diversion, or con-
	8	versation; examination of the day.
	9	
Evening question, What good have I done today?	10	
	11	
	12	
	1	Sleep.
	2	
	3	
	4	

To tie all of the productivity points together, here's what my routine has looked like for the last couple years. (Yes, being a morning person helps!)

4:00 a.m. – Wake (without an alarm!) and immediately meditate for 25 minutes.

4:30 a.m. – Eat breakfast, read The Wall Street Journal, review and take quick action on emails from overnight,

5:00 a.m. – Review my journal, determine and record the Big Three Things for the day, record gratitude and write down any other thoughts.

5:15 a.m. – Begin the Hour of Power with the most difficult of the Big Three Things.

6:15 a.m. – Go to the gym for an hour. Strength work three days a week, cardio and CrossFit class three days a week, one day of rest.

7:30 a.m. – Say good morning to my wife! Connect and discuss the day. Communication and respect!

7:55 a.m. – Go into the office. (Yes, I'm lucky—my office is at home.)

8:00 a.m. – Handle any necessary early discussions with the team. Otherwise, continue working on the Big Three Things.

8:30 a.m. – Morning video conference with the team.

8:45 a.m. – Begin pomodoro sequence until 11:30am, turning off distractions and taking a break every 50 minutes. After the Hour of Power, this is my most productive time.

11:30 a.m. – Break for lunch. Get out of the office, perhaps take a kinhin meditation on the beach or a half-hour nap.

12:30 p.m. – 5:00 p.m. – This is my least productive time of the day, so I try to schedule phone calls and other non- project work during this time. I will also run personal errands if necessary.

5:00 p.m. – 7:00 p.m. – Eat dinner with my wife. Focus on mindfully connecting. No computer, phone, or television!

7:00 p.m. – 9:30 p.m. – Catch up on reading. I've found it very difficult to work on projects at this time, so I use it to read something different.

9:30 p.m. – Reflect on the day, sometimes on the back patio under the stars. Review my journal and make initial plans for tomorrow.

10:00 p.m. – To bed.

Create Flow

If you are interested in something, you will focus on it,
and if you focus attention on anything, it is likely that you will
become interested in it.
– Mihaly Csíkszentmihályi

Those of us in the Lean world are accustomed to discussing "flow," where work is performed in a steady manner to reduce unevenness (*mura*). Activities are synchronized, layouts are optimized, and resources are available exactly where and when they are needed in order to match the pace set by the true demand for a product or service. The operation just hums along creating value for the customer. Well, "just" is a bit of a misnomer, as achieving flow can be very difficult.

The concept of flow was developed by Mihaly Csíkszentmihályi, a psychologist of Hungarian descent and professor at Claremont Graduate University. (I remember being introduced to Csíkszentmihályi's work decades ago in a psychology class, and have recently become reacquainted with him while researching motivation and productivity.) Csíkszentmihályi describes flow as being completely absorbed by what you are doing, and energized, with the creative juices flowing. Similarly, he once explained flow as "being completely involved in an activity for its own sake. The ego falls away. Time flies. Every action, movement, and thought follows inevitably from the previous one, like playing jazz. Your whole being is involved, and you're using your skills to the utmost." Many of us think of flow as "being in the zone." It is truly a positive, invigorating experience, as opposed to "hyperfocus," which can be negative.

Flow has parallels with concepts in religion and philosophy. Buddhism talks about "action with inaction" and Taoism has "doing without doing. The Hindu Ashtavakra Gita and Bhagavad-Gita have similar descriptions. Hippocrates said "there is one common flow, one common breathing, all things are in sympathy."

Csíkszentmihályi began researching the concept out of a fascination with artists and other professionals who became so engrossed in their work that they forgot about everything else, sometimes even basic needs such as food or sleep. Components of flow include a challenge-skill balance (when a person's skill level is nearly equal to the difficulty of the task at hand), the merging of action and awareness, clarity of goals, immediate and unambiguous feedback, concentration on the task, transformation of time, and the autotelic experience. Flow happens when the necessary skill level and challenge environment are high. The ability to be creative and accomplished in such a situation is very fulfilling.

Is Csíkszentmihályi's flow different than Lean flow? Maybe not. Completely involved, every action following inevitably from the previous, using skills to the utmost, clarity of goals, immediate feedback, curiosity, humility—to me, it sounds like a finely-tuned manufacturing or office work cell.

The comparison has merit. In addition to his research on flow from an individual perspective, Csíkszentmihályi also researched "group flow," where both individuals as well as the group are able to achieve flow. The characteristics of group flow are:

- Workplace reconfigurability, mostly standing.
- Charts for information inputs, flowcharts, project summaries, results, open topics, and parking lots.
- Organized work cells.
- Experimentation.
- Visual controls of process, movement, and status.

The use of visual controls, open and transparent communication, and experimentation also add to the similarities between flow and Lean. One of the reasons Lean work cells perform well is that they create a fulfilling, productive, and improving operation by leveraging and rewarding the brains of humans, helping them to reach a state of flow as they do their work. When this happens, the operation does hum along and create value for the customer.

Part Four – Lead

To handle yourself, use your head; to handle others, use your heart.
- Eleanor Roosevelt

Now that you have worked on understanding yourself and improving your productivity, future tools and concepts will be more easily applied to both personal and professional leadership situations. On the professional side, you'll need to work with your team; therefore, let's look at some ways to effectively lead people.

Key Points from this Section:
- Leading people is just that: leading people.
- Trust can be a powerful motivator for your team. It requires authenticity, humility, and a lack of fear.
- Respect also means listening mindfully, sharing, and mentoring.
- Create a high-performance organization by hiring high-performance people, then respecting them to do the right thing.
- Don't forget to also lead and respect yourself.

Oh the Humanity!

When we treat people merely as they are, they will remain as they are. When we treat them as if they were what they should be, they will become what they should be.
– *Thomas S. Monson*

We're supposedly all human, but sometimes we don't act that way. Traditional leadership thinking has taught us that it is acceptable, sometimes even expected, for leaders to be harsh, uncaring, and distant. We may even believe that improving the bottom line means making choices such as putting the organization ahead of individuals.

Traditional business accounting skews our perspective to think of people only as costs. Nowhere on a profit and loss statement is the value of employee creativity, knowledge, and experience explicitly stated. This leads managers to make crazy decisions, like shedding thousands of years of experience in order to achieve a couple bucks an hour of labor cost savings.

Being a leader (instead of just a manager) means you should think differently. Human-centric leadership recognizes that your people are human and they should be valued accordingly. By understanding this, you can promote and get the most out the human side of your organization, your team, or even your family.

Respect

If you want to be respected, you must respect yourself.
– Spanish Proverb

Respect for people is one of the two pillars of Lean. However, "people" doesn't just mean the people that report to you, but everyone else in your organization, including your team, your boss, your customers, your suppliers, your community, and yourself. The "respect for people" concept from Toyota is more accurately translated as "respect for humanity."

To respect people, you must take into account that there is a brain attached to each pair of hands in your company. In addition to the cost of the pair of hands that is represented on traditional financial statements, those brains hold tremendous value. As a leader, your job is to figure out what environment, both physical and organizational, is necessary to optimize and leverage that value. You increase the value by soliciting and using people's ideas, creativity, experience, and knowledge.

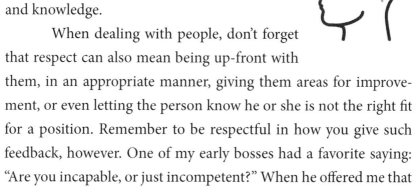

When dealing with people, don't forget that respect can also mean being up-front with them, in an appropriate manner, giving them areas for improvement, or even letting the person know he or she is not the right fit for a position. Remember to be respectful in how you give such feedback, however. One of my early bosses had a favorite saying: "Are you incapable, or just incompetent?" When he offered me that choice, I didn't know what to say. But I did know I wouldn't grow in such an environment, so I soon left to join a different company on the other side of the country. (The man treated everyone, high performers and otherwise, with such disdain, and wondered why his group had such high—and expensive—turnover.)

We must also remember to treat people with dignity. A couple years ago, I read an article on the power of calling people by their names. Using someone's name creates a connection that can be very powerful. Instead of yelling "hey you!" to someone, learn their name and use it to address them. When you write emails, greet them before launching into the subject. Do the same when talking in person and on the phone. Great leaders are able to connect with their workers by taking a little time to acknowledge them first, before getting down to business.

Empathy and Compassion

Resolve to be tender with the young, compassionate with the aged, sympathetic with the striving, and tolerant of the weak and the wrong. Sometime in life you will have been all of these.
– Lloyd Shearer

About fifteen years into my career, I thought of myself as a strong manager. I had progressed up the ranks and was responsible for an entire telecom equipment manufacturing facility, leveraging Lean with a great group of people.

Then the demand for our product went off a cliff. One day, the vice president I reported to visited from headquarters, gathered all two hundred of us in a room, and proceeded to say, "My spreadsheet says this operation is no longer viable, therefore I am shutting it down." Then he left and went back to his office 250 miles away.

In all honesty, I knew the closure was coming. I had taken part in many meetings trying to figure out an alternative, but demand really had dried up, almost overnight. Management had little choice but to make the tough decision to close the facility.

But the decision did not need to be communicated this way.

Understandably, my team was very upset. They knew times were tough, but they didn't know this decision was coming so fast. They didn't want to hear that a spreadsheet had determined their fate. They wanted to hear how difficult it was, at least for me, to make the decision. And they wanted some understanding and recognition of how hard it would be for them and their families.

Unfortunately, things would get worse before they got better. The next day was September 11th, 2001. In one day, the world changed and we became even more fearful, while still processing the previous day's announcement that everyone had lost their jobs.

Our site leadership team's response was a bit different from corporate headquarters' response. We had long thought of our employees as part of our family, and we were empathetic and compassionate. We became completely transparent about the process, what had happened, and what we could do to help the employees until the closure date. We made special accommodations for some, helped others with their job searches, and simply listened, mindfully, to everyone. The employees recognized this and realized they could trust us, and that we would work for their best interests. Although it didn't change the eventual outcome, we were able to execute a complex facility closure in a professional and human-centered manner. Many of us remain friends and even colleagues to this day.

The lesson of this experience helped me several times later on when we had to make difficult but necessary decisions that negatively impacted people. By treating people like people (as I would like to be treated), truly listening to them and understanding their needs and fears, we made bad situations better. Most of all, we created trust in our organization's leadership.

Humility

Remain humble. Don't worry about who receives the credit. Never let power or authority go to your head.
– Dick Winters, Beyond Band of Brothers

Arrogance and ego have ruined many a leader. Unfortunately, these characteristics are still accepted today, although they shouldn't be. If your goal is to optimize the value of your people, thereby improving the value of your organization, then you need to support and nurture them. You have to admit that you cannot know or control everything that happens and be humble enough to trust others to do their jobs.

Humility means accepting that you're human and that you have faults, vulnerabilities, and worries like everyone else. Humble leaders are actually more confident than ego-driven leaders, as they are secure enough to show and admit their vulnerabilities and even mistakes. They are open to alternative ideas because they know, understand, and respect that they don't have all the answers. (Examples of successful CEOs that take a more humble approach include Jeff Bezos of Amazon and Tony Hsei of Zappos.) This creates confidence, and thereby motivation, within the organization. Humble leaders let people do their jobs, aren't afraid to ask stupid questions, turn mistakes into learning and mentoring opportunities, encourage dissent and embrace opinions and methods different than their own, and forego the trappings of power.

Years ago, when I was named president of the medical device company I ended up leading for eight years, my very first action—within the first hour of starting the job—was to remove the "Reserved for President" parking spot. Later, I removed the custom furniture from my office, and when we built a new building, I ditched the private bathroom. These were small actions in the grand scheme of things, but they sent a message to the company that I was no better than others who worked there.

The approach paid dividends several years later, when I needed considerable time off and flexibility to deal with a family medical situation. I was open with my team about what was going on and I received incredible support, understanding, and compassion from them.

95

Do you display arrogance or ego at home or in the workplace? Would your family or coworkers agree? What would happen if you made your vulnerabilities and shortcomings more visible? How would your peers, team, and family react?

Share Generously

Teaching is a gift you give not only to others, but also to yourself.
You give and you receive, you teach and you learn.
– Andrea Goeglein

When I became president of the medical device company, I already had a decade of Lean experience. I knew what fundamentals needed to be put in place, what systems needed improvement, and what knowledge needed to be transferred.

Instead of ordering this or that program to be implemented, I decided to help the team identify problems and point them to potential solutions. For example, when we were taking too much time to find production supplies, I suggested they consider using a Lean concept known as 5S. Instead of teaching them everything myself, I let the team take charge of implementing it. The team embraced this management style: first they learned about 5S, and then they implemented what they learned. We repeated this process with several other Lean concepts. They would go and learn about it, and I would coach them on implementation. I shared my knowledge and experience, but a funny thing happened along the way: the team also taught me some new methods they had identified and developed.

In the end, there were still a couple of changes I needed to dictate, one being the morning standup meeting. The team did not think that adding a new daily meeting would be beneficial. But when I made the meeting mandatory, I also let them know exactly why it was being done, why it was important to me, and what results we should expect from it. Within a few weeks they also saw the value, and I know that it continues to this day, more than three years after I left the company.

Another thing we did at the company was to emphasize employee training. People want to learn, and it's a measure of your respect for them (and their brains) that you provide opportunities for them to learn. I've seen far too many organizations that believe it is too expensive to send employees to conferences, workshops, and other events. Yes, it costs money, but those folks come back motivated and wanting to improve! Isn't that worth a couple grand? If you cannot recapture the investment of a conference or workshop, you aren't asking enough of your team.

Every year, I sent quite a few employees to events, choosing people that had demonstrated a passion for learning as well as some that I thought could learn a lot if they were appropriately motivated and respected. In each case, I asked them to come back with three to five ideas that we should implement now, as well as three to five ideas that were pretty cool and we should keep in mind for the future. They presented these ideas to our leadership team as a group, and it was then up to us to evaluate and implement them. The process was difficult, but the new ideas easily paid for the trips, many times over. Properly nurtured, the employees who had gone to the trainings became forceful proponents for improvement.

Sharing your knowledge and experience doesn't just have to be within your organization. One of my most rewarding activities is writing the blog I started over ten years ago. My posts have ranged across many topics, some far outside of Lean, but the response I've received has been tremendous. I've also met some incredible people who have become very valuable friends and colleagues—some are now business partners. The effort has also improved my writing ability and helped me organize my thoughts, which eventually even led to this book!

I've also learned a lot about recruiting over the years. I've had several failures where professionals with great experience and resumes ended up not being the right fit. I have learned that the best predictor of executive success, more than experience, education, references, or personality, is the ability to share and teach new knowledge. More specifically, executives should have a craving for new knowledge, the capability to distill the knowledge, and an ability to effectively share the knowledge. Those types of individuals are few and far between, but they are incredibly valuable and can radically change an organization.

To respect people, you must recognize and leverage the potential value of people's brains. To optimize that value, you must share your experience, skills, and knowledge. Sharing is respecting people.

Serve

True leadership must be for the benefit of the followers, not the enrichment of the leaders.
– Robert Townsend

Servant leadership has unfortunately become something of a leadership buzzword, yet the concept is sound. Building off of respect, humility, and trust, the servant leader truly thinks of him or herself differently. Instead of being at the top of the pyramid, they are at the bottom. Their job is to serve the organization, their team, or their family by enabling the success of others. By doing so, they enable the success of the organization.

Servant leaders ignite the passion in an organization by drawing the human connection to the task or goal. They unite people rather than place them into silos. They sacrifice when the going gets tough, and this earns them the respect and commitment of the organization.

You may find it hard to think of examples of servant leaders, because most do not desire fame, accolades, or prizes and are therefore not often in the public eye. Two servant leaders who did become famous are Abraham Lincoln and Dr. Martin Luther King, Jr. President Lincoln could have taken the easy route and let the Union dissolve or simply let slavery remain intact. However he took

99

the far more difficult path because he knew it would be better in the long run for the people he was serving. Dr. King eschewed recognition and desired to be remembered for helping drive social justice. He also took the harder approach to creating change by promoting non-violence. Nelson Mandela, Mahatma Gandhi, and Mother Teresa are other examples.

Incredible people, but anyone can be a servant leader.

What would happen in your organization, in your team, or even in your family if you acted like a servant instead of a boss? How would that make you feel? Where and how can you enable success by working to enable the success of others?

Authentic Character

The time is always right to do what is right.
– Martin Luther King, Jr.

A mindful leader has awakened to his or her true meaning, purpose, and values. Hopefully, those values align with a strong sense of integrity, character, passion, and people-centered leadership. The authentic leader takes these values and overtly leads with them.

The people surrounding and working for an authentic leader recognize and witness the values of that leader every day. They know the leader genuinely believes in and lives those values, both at work and at home. In Zen, this authenticity and naturalness is shizen. Shizen inspires confidence in followers, leading to increased motivation and better performance. Authentic leaders truly lead. They are the first ones to go into battle, and they focus on building up their own troops. They take risks, and explain the reason for the risks as well as the possible consequences. The authentic leader leads with character and integrity.

However, being authentic does not mean that you should embrace your inner jerk or narcissist. It also does not mean you should be inflexible. Authentic leadership is built on character, not style, and is flexible to fit the situation and capabilities of the team.

Character matters, especially in leadership. We've seen many examples where character flaws compromise effective leadership, politicians and otherwise. I was disappointed when the constituents of each of them tried to excuse the behavior as part of their personal life and not representative of their professional leadership. Sorry, that doesn't fly.

There is no great wall between personal and professional leadership. Both are directly interrelated and aligned, which is exactly why this book focuses on both. A leader without personal character cannot be a great professional leader. Character is not divisible. Thought patterns in the brain are not divisible. You cannot say a person has a high level of character in one area and then forgive a lack of character in another. You cannot say a person can make great decisions in one aspect of life and be a complete idiot in another. It's the same brain. Choices are made consciously, and when a seemingly upstanding leader makes poor decisions, the evidence points directly at a lack of character. (It is important to note that there are cultural considerations with character. The personal follies of leaders may be issues in one culture, but not in others. However, an authentic leader is also aware of context, and

101

leads accordingly, without narcissism and intellectual dishonesty.) Mahatma Gandhi once said "Your beliefs become your thoughts, Your thoughts become your words, Your words become your actions, Your actions become your habits, Your habits become your values, Your values become your destiny."

Zen builds character by removing and controlling people's material and superficial desires. As D.T. Suzuki writes in *Essays on Zen Buddhism*: "Zen may be considered a discipline aiming at the reconstruction of character. Our ordinary life only touches the fringe of personality, it does not cause a commotion in the deepest parts of the soul. We are made to live on the superficiality of things. We may be clever, bright, and all that, but what we produce lacks depth, sincerity, and does not appeal to the inmost feelings. A deep spiritual experience is bound to effect a change in the moral structure of one's personality."

Like all of us, I'm not perfect. I've wronged people and made the occasional poor choice. But I learned my lessons. When I moved into a leadership position, I received the trust of others and very consciously began to hold myself to a higher standard. I deeply felt that trust and responsibility, from when I had just one direct report to when I had a thousand. My decisions and actions, both personal and professional, influenced and affected lives and livelihoods. I soon realized that in my personal life, I had leadership responsibilities of a different form and should hold myself to higher standards at all times.

When a leader's weaknesses are exposed, it becomes an opportunity for the leader to demonstrate authentic leadership. At that moment, he has the opportunity to show us what we should do when we are faced with our own shortcomings and mistakes. This creates trust. However, when a leader tries to cover up his weaknesses, lie about them or blame others, he demonstrates that he does not have the character to be a leader.

Is your leadership style and method overtly aligned with your values and principles? Do your team members, including your friends and family, experience your values every time they interact with you? Are you unwavering in those principles? When you make a mistake, do you admit them, learn, and change?

Communication, Not Structure

When the trust account is high, communication
is easy, instant, and effective.
– Stephen R. Covey

Changing an organization's structure seems to be the common knee-jerk response to internal issues. My prior company embarked on a reorganization to eliminate arbitrary site- and function-based structures so that we could align around corporate-wide value creation processes.

During the restructuring process, an organization typically inserts a new management layer, such as a Chief Operating Officer (COO). Think about this from a "respect for people" perspective. The now-lower heads of each functional group no longer receive the mentoring of the CEO. They have been diminished in stature, and their voices and concerns have to go through another layer to be heard by top management. This is not likely to solve any of the

103

internal problems facing a company.

If you look at the root causes to internal problems, you'll often find that certain groups and their leaders aren't communicating effectively. They aren't aligned, and changing the organizational structure will not change that one iota. In fact, it will just shift the problem around and probably create new troubles.

Years ago, I was having similar issues in my company. Leaders weren't leading, they weren't talking, and they weren't aligned. Different levels of commitment and different interpersonal communication styles were causing misunderstandings, leading to quality and customer issues. So we took the entire extended executive leadership team through Patrick Lencioni's *The Five Dysfunctions of a Team* and accompanying workbooks. Over the course of a year, we addressed our absence of trust, misalignment, communication, and the like.

Sometimes the training was very difficult, like the exercise where each member of the leadership team stood up and listened while the others openly and candidly discussed their "areas for improvement." We nearly lost a couple team members that day. But in the end, our leadership team learned how to openly and honestly communicate, which helped us align ourselves with one another. (Later, we found we needed to work hard to sustain this improvement; otherwise, we'd lapse into traditional silo politics.)

The second thing we did to improve the leadership team happened by accident. We had to demolish one of our new buildings to make room for a new facility, and during the two-year construction period, I moved my leadership team into a triple-wide trailer. We planted a couple of pink flamingos out front and nicknamed it the "Flamingo Hilton." The new office was uncomfortable and the walls were paper-thin. We had to learn to live close together and deal with the conversations we heard on the other sides of the walls. The proximity, though not always fun, improved our communication. The daily executive leadership team standup meeting, where we video conferenced with the leadership of our other sites, also helped.

The lessons we learned in the trailer changed how we planned our company's future. As we were designing our new facility, we had a lot of debate about where the senior leadership team members should reside. Initially, I favored an approach that is common in Lean environments, where each leadership team member is with his or her team, often on the production floor itself. However, we decided to go against Lean convention and locate the senior leadership team together on the second floor of the building. One big reason for this was that we noticed when a senior leadership team member spent too much time with his team, the supervisory and decision-making capability of junior leaders suffered. As much as we tried to encourage younger leaders to take initiative, it was just too easy to revert to the senior manager making the decisions. One set of stairs removed the temptation for upper management to get involved when it shouldn't, thereby creating respect for our people by enabling their independence, autonomy, and growth. Additionally, we found it was easier to focus the senior leadership team on future strategy instead of the day-to-day mayhem.

Physically separating the executive and junior management workspaces did not prevent senior team members from spending a lot of time mentoring, teaching, and helping their teams. But the small change in our physical location, which changed our focus and perspective, was important. Our junior leaders learned to step up and make decisions, eventually adding a lot of leadership strength to our company.

As we learned, simply changing the structure of an organization does not create excellence and effectiveness. You have to dig deep to improve the underlying leadership competence and communication. As you do that, the organizational structure becomes less and less relevant.

When you find your company is not producing the results you want, it may be time for some big changes, but not the ones you think. Instead of reorganizing your corporate structure, first look to solve conflict issues by improving leadership capability and communication—not by adding a new layer of management. Respect your managers by providing training, mentoring, and feedback to improve their leadership skills. Respect your managers by allowing them to interact across a wide span, and be mentored by senior leaders. Respect others in the organization by reducing layers and barriers to communication, and you will be much more likely to produce the changes you are looking for.

Trust, Not Control

If you live your life honestly and truthfully, you'll be open and transparent, which leads to trust.
– Dalai Lama

It is common for better leaders to take a step back from the perils of micromanagement, but in many organizations, controlling managers are still accepted and even expected. When we attempt to control every scenario and possible outcome, we fall into a bottomless "what if" pit and end up spending more time and effort on contingency plans than we would to handle an unexpected situation. At the same time, over-managed employees feel undervalued—an accurate assumption, since in control environments the power of their brains is not being utilized to its potential.

The purpose of a leader is to define and manage principles and vision. In effect, a leader's job is to create the guardrails of the wide superhighway, not to drive the car. Respect your employees by giving them the control to develop and execute the plans required to drive down the highway. Mentor and provide oversight, but don't try to execute others' jobs. Allowing employees to do their jobs requires trust and acceptance that there may be multiple ways to complete a task. Providing a safe environment for managers to take acceptable risks and to make the occasional failure creates learning opportunities and growth, another aspect of respect for people.

You can also create trust by being authentic, which I already discussed. Listen without judgment and engage in real discussion.

Hold yourself to a high character, ethical, and moral standard, and admit when you fail. Model good behavior and do what you say you will. Know what matters and show appreciation in a way that impacts people as individuals.

When I was dealing with the difficult family medical situation and had to be out of the office for a couple weeks at a time, often unable to even have phone conversations, I had to trust my team to manage a complex business. They did fine without me. Sure, I might have done some things differently, but not necessarily more optimally. Occasionally, the guardrails had to be tweaked or narrowed, but it was rare. How liberating it was for me, during that time of crisis and afterwards, to be able to trust my team!

You might be surprised to hear that you can lead better, personally and professionally, by doing less. Think about what more you could accomplish by relinquishing control and trusting others to do their jobs. Can the value of leadership be redefined so less is actually more?

Performance, Not Policy

Few people realize how employee policy manuals, usually given to you on your first day and then mostly forgotten, shape an organization's culture and thereby its fundamental performance.

To give you a reference point, one company I worked for had a forty-plus-page employee manual that started every section with "COMPLIANCE IS ESSENTIAL" highlighted in bold, with "required to conform" sprinkled liberally throughout the document. The manual ended with a meaty discussion of the punitive measures that would happen if someone deviated from the policies. And this was a company considered very innovative in many ways!

The other extreme is Zaarly, a San Francisco-based startup. Its employee handbook, posted online for even non-employees to see, talks directly about culture. The "Rules for Work" section begins with "We don't have these." And in a style prevalent throughout the document, it adds that "if you want to coast, we recommend you apply for a job at Craigslist." Included are some good thoughts on teams, work, and communication, but no rules.

Another example is the famous Netflix "business culture" PowerPoint that serves as the company's employee handbook. Similar to Zaarly's handbook, it talks a lot about culture and a lack of rules. There is no vacation policy, and the travel and expense policy is literally five words: "Act in Netflix's best interests." That's it. Unlike Zaarly, Netflix does say some rules are necessary, such as: "Absolutely no harassment of any kind." In this case, I completely agree, especially on that item. Some topics relating to privacy, security, and regulatory requirements are important enough that they need to be spelled out in no uncertain terms.

Netflix believes high-performance people should be free to make decisions, and those decisions need to be grounded in context. Mission, vision, and value statements do not create context. To demonstrate this, Netflix's presentation provides the example of how Enron's value statement included "integrity." Real company values are shown by who gets rewarded for embodying desired behaviors and skills. The document goes on to describe the primary Netflix values and the associated behaviors.

At Netflix, flexibility is more important over the long term than efficiency. To inhibit the chaos that too much flexibility in a large organization can create, the company hires (and keeps) only high-performance people. High-performance people make great decisions, so building a staff of them is better than having people who are good at following lists of rules. Later on in the Netflix document, there is a good discussion that encourages managing with context instead of trying to control people. That way, when something fails, managers look to figure out what went wrong with the process rather than with the people.

One part of the Netflix document that gave me pause was an insinuation that defined processes (such as standard work) are all bad. But doing standard work doesn't necessarily mean the employee has zero flexibility. As those of us in the Lean world know, standard work is the foundation for kaizen. Once an employee deeply understands a process, he or she can (and is expected to) come up with ways to improve it and then share it, which is called *yokoten.*

In January 2014, Brad Power posted a piece in Harvard Business Review titled *Drive Performance by Focusing on Routine Decisions* that hits at a similar concept. Instead of creating rule-bound defined processes, companies should focus on improving the quality of the decisions made by managers. Power illustrates the idea with an example those of us in the manufacturing world have all experienced: the maelstrom of materials control. He describes how the materials department of an electronics distributor was able to improve operations by better training managers to make key decisions about inventory. The goal of the training was to get managers to focus less on perfecting company processes (the "box and arrows" of a flowchart) and more on understanding what objectives the processes were supporting in the first place. When managers were able to understand how the processes affected actual business performance, they were able to make decisions (the "diamonds and arrows") that improved performance:

> These two stories highlight the advantages of focusing process improvement on "diamonds and arrows" — i.e., making better decisions. Project leaders who focus exclusively on the "boxes and arrows" of workflow action improvement will often find themselves caught up fixing yesterday's operations and systems issues. Workers who participate in these interviews and workshops tend to fixate on the pain points they want fixed. This focus on immediate problems can actually distract the project team from the real goals of the business and the decisions that will help achieve them.

Are your rules improving the boxes (company processes) but harming the diamonds (managers' decision-making)? How is that rigidity affecting your long-term performance? Do you have a team of high-performance people that you can trust to deal with the diamonds in a flexible, agile way? And how do your underlying documents, even down to the employee handbook, support or impede that? These are questions to consider as you look to improve your company's performance.

111

Coaching, Not Reviews

A coach is someone who can give correction
without causing resentment.
– John Wooden

We all dislike the traditional performance review. Employees hate going in for them and managers hate writing them. Traditional performance reviews are 90% rearview mirror and 10% (if you're lucky) discussion about the future. But feedback is still critically important, so what should take the place of the traditional review?

Instead of using traditional reviews, many Lean organizations use a technique called coaching kata, which Mike Rother describes in his book, *Toyota Kata*. A kata is a small routine that you repeat over time until it becomes a habit. In his book, Rother focuses on two types of kata: *improvement kata and coaching kata*

The first step in implementing kata is identifying the *target condition* (not the same as a goal). The target condition is the behavior or capability that is ultimately desired; therefore, it is more than an intermediate improvement point or goal—even if that point represents a significant improvement. The next step is to identify the *actual condition*, which is the person's current behavior or capability. Once those two end points are known, the person imagines what obstacles might impede achieving the target condition. The obstacles are not ranked or prioritized, but are simply identified.

Once the obstacles are identified, the next step is to create an experiment to overcome them, one at a time. The experiment could include some form of additional training, a tweak to some behavior, and so forth. If the experiment is successful, it becomes part of the new standard. If not, the learner analyzes what went wrong and tries a new one. Each of these experiments should be fairly small and rapid, creating ongoing forward movement with little downside risk of failure.

These experiments are monitored by the team member's supervisor in a process known as coaching kata. The coaching kata activity creates ongoing improvement opportunities for both team leaders and team members. Managers, acting as coaches, ask their employees a series of questions to help them understand how their actual condition compares to their target condition. Then, the team member identifies—with coaching support from the leader—small experiments to overcome the next obstacle. The team member evaluates the results of the experiment and creates a conclusion, which is then reviewed with the leader to identify the next experiment for improvement. This process helps managers reinforce the patterns that workers learn from their improvement kata.

Instead of the once-a-year ordeal that is common with performance reviews, coaching kata creates an ongoing coaching relationship between managers and workers. It helps them continually improve while pursuing an agreed-upon target condition. Expectations are clear for everyone, which shows respect for the employees and produces better results for the company

Joy, Not Fear

Those whose minds are shaped by selfless thoughts
give joy when they speak or act.
– Buddha

A couple years ago, I heard about a remarkable company, Menlo Innovations, created by a remarkable leader, Richard Sheridan. Gemba Academy sent a video team to talk to him and see his company in action, and what we learned was truly inspirational. Sheridan built the company on a unique foundation: to create *joy*. Although it is a software design firm, everything the company does is done to add joy to the lives of its customers and employees. Menlo's mission is to "end human suffering as it relates to software."

According to Sheridan, the key to create joy for your customers is to create joy for your employees. To create joy for your employees, you must lead without creating fear. Fear comes from a lack of trust, which can be a problem when information isn't available, when job expectations are not clear, when there isn't enough time or support to be able to do a good job. Fear reduces a person's ability to access the brain's prefrontal cortex, rendering the person unable to take full advantage of creativity, innovation, and rational thought.

Menlo Innovations works to remove the sources of fear. First and foremost, the company's leaders are authentic and trusted. The hiring process is lengthy and grueling to ensure new team members will support and thrive in the Menlo culture. Financial and other business information is openly shared, posted, and discussed, to a depth that would easily scare the traditional CFO. The company eliminated most meetings, and those that remain must add significant value. The objectives, responsibilities, and status of every project are also posted—clarity created by visual management. Employees work in teams of two, allowing them to provide mutual support, relief, and coaching. The transparency about the status of the company and current projects eliminates ambiguity and thereby reduces the fear of uncertainty.

Work to create joy, not fear, by being open, authentic, and trustworthy. Support your team members by providing the time, resources, training, and expectations necessary for them to do their jobs. Your customers will thank you.

Listen Deeply and Speak Softly

Learn to be quiet enough to hear the sound of the genuine within yourself so that you can hear it in others.
– Marian Wright Edelman

A common problem with leaders, especially as they transition to new leadership roles, is that they do not listen to others very well. Leaders typically progress by speaking up and being noticed, and the shift from speaking to listening is difficult.

Truly listening requires being very present, aware, and mindful of what the other person is saying. While someone else is talking, don't think of what they have to say as a pause between what you said before and what you want to say when the person is done. Don't check your phone or think about other projects. Just listen. Ask questions that encourage dialogue on the topic, not just short responses. At the end of the conversation, reflect on what was said and what you learned, and be open to changing your previous opinion and perceptions. If appropriate, communicate how you plan to respond, and follow up to demonstrate that the person's ideas are important to you.

Similarly, communicate openly and transparently, but softly and only when necessary. A hallmark of the best leaders I've been lucky to work with is that they are often the quietest people in the room. They don't feel the need to assert their authority by talking, as they have already earned it with their authenticity. When you speak, every word should be necessary and have meaning. Being concise is powerful, and it respects the time of others. Think about and plan everything you say, but keep your message real and authentic.

One of the realities of being a leader is that we have to deal with conflicts—between coworkers, between peers, or even with our spouses or other family members. Most of us do not enjoy conflict, and a typical response is to clam up or make a hasty decision. We will do anything to resolve the situation quickly so we can move on to more fun tasks, like analyzing our department's profit and loss statement.

Mindful leadership requires a different approach. Respect the other person, or the people with the conflict, by truly listening. Don't assume you understand the context and their perspective. Ask questions to get to the root cause. Display humility, and put yourself in the servant position trying to enable the success of the people and organization. Be authentic by reinforcing your values and principles. Remember that solutions don't have to be win-lose. By doing this, you can get rid of your fear of conflict, and even reduce the amount of conflict within your organization. Your team, knowing that their views are heard, considered, and respected, will be more open and accepting to your eventual decision, even if it conflicts with what they believe.

And Then There's You

Rest and self-care are so important. When you take time to replenish your spirit, it allows you to serve others from the overflow. You cannot serve from an empty vessel.
– Eleanor Brown

Up to this point, I've talked a lot about teams, organizations, and family. Don't forget that you are also human and have needs, desires, and vulnerabilities. Respect yourself, trust yourself, and be authentic to yourself.

Caregivers know that you can't effectively take care of others if you don't first take care of yourself. The principle is the same one that applies to the oxygen masks on planes. You put yours on first, then help others with theirs. Aid workers in disaster zones are told to go into the tent and eat, even if others around them are starving. It can be tough for leaders focused on enabling their teams through human-centered leadership to do this, but sometimes you have to put yourself first.

Feeling run down, either mentally or physically? Perhaps you need a vacation or some time away to rejuvenate. Take the time to exercise and focus on your health. Embrace some solitude to allow your thoughts to settle. Whatever it takes, recognize and accept that you are human too. Your team will notice your authenticity and support you.

Part Five – Clarify

Clarity of purpose,
Clarity of understanding.
– Zen saying

Now it's time to analyze your organization and develop a clear plan for improvement. I want you to consider doing this for your own personal improvement as well. What are your values? How do you want to change? What plans can you create?

Key Points from this Section:
- Determine the principles and values of your organization and yourself.
- Determine why you want to accomplish something in order to give your endeavors purpose.
- Observe and document your current state, then develop your desired future state.
- From the gaps between the current state and future state, create a hoshin plan with long-term objectives, breakthrough objectives, and annual goals.
- Document your plans on A3 reports.

119

Define Principles and Values

In matters of style, swim with the current;
in matters of principle, stand like a rock.
– Thomas Jefferson

Many organizations jump to trying to write down their vision or mission statement before taking the time to really think about and define their core principles. Principles are the foundation upon which the company is built and (hopefully) operates. They are so important that you should be willing to sacrifice significant business, or even the company itself, to preserve the principle.

In private companies and smaller organizations, the principles often come from the values of the owners or founders. For example, a company I used to work for was owned by a couple of devout Catholics. Because of this, the entire organization knew there were some products that we would not make for any price because they conflicted with Catholic beliefs. The employees fully supported that principle, even though it cost the company business.

I'm very proud that the company I co-founded, Gemba Academy, values ethics, integrity, and respect for people above all else. We know our success is built on the efforts and creativity of our people. We respect our people by having an unlimited vacation policy, being transparent with our business operations, and, for a very small company, having a strong benefits package that includes health care, 401(k), and profit sharing. This respect extends to our customers too. We've had situations where customers wanted to purchase a product, but we knew it wasn't the right fit for them. We openly told them, demonstrating respect for the customers and our values.

Think about your personal principles and values. What do you truly care about? Your principles should be so important that you'd be willing to give up business—such as not taking a job, even if your livelihood depended on it—to not cross them. Bill George, former CEO of Medtronic and currently a professor at Harvard, calls this the True North, or inner compass. Principles are important because they create the perspective, boundaries, and culture for the organization. Without them, there is a good chance that the culture will evolve on its own, based on the values of the stronger-willed employees.

What are the core principles and values of your organization and yourself?

What's Your Why?

Make your work to be in keeping with your purpose.
– Leonardo da Vinci

Vision and mission statements have long been the rage in organizations as they supposedly define what the organization is about. Do you know what your organization's vision or mission is? Could you tell me what either one is, right now—without looking it up? I thought not. I bet they're hanging on the wall in some conference room, gathering dust. Unfortunately, this is all too common.

121

Another problem with vision and mission statements is that the terms themselves aren't very clear and create confusion. Employees always seem to wonder what the difference between the vision and mission is. Also, the mission statement of the company often does not reflect the reality of what the company is trying to create. I've seen many cases where the true mission of a company was to make money and the vision was to make a lot of money. Seriously.

This is why I prefer a purpose, or "why?" statement. I believe it is far clearer in terms of definition, and therefore easier to own and promote. Why did you create your company? Why does it exist? What problem are you trying to solve?

The why? of Gemba Academy is to "remove the struggle of continuous improvement training." It's simple, but it says a lot. We started the company to help smaller organizations that otherwise could not access high quality continuous improvement training, but we also include large multinationals that are struggling to deploy training across global locations.

Like many other organizations that use a purpose statement instead of a vision statement, we also have a mission that further defines what we are trying to accomplish. Our mission statement talks about how we create high-quality content, then we help organizations undertake and sustain their continuous improvement journeys.

The ideas behind these statements are only useful if a company puts them into practice, and to achieve this, everyone in an organization needs to be involved. Although the founders, owners, and leadership team often work to create an organization's principles, *why?*, and mission, it is important to engage employees by involving them in the planning process (we'll discuss this in more detail in the Create the Hoshin Plan section). By doing so, you create acceptance, ownership, and understanding of the foundational statements. Then everyone can use the same core set of principles, the same *why?* statement, and the same mission statement to review and analyze your organization.

Going beyond your organization, what about you? What is your purpose, your *why?* Cornell University researchers recently confirmed that a sense of purpose decreases impulsivity, thereby making choices that pay of better in the long term. This is something to contemplate on your next seijaku (quietude) experience.

The Beginner's Mind

In the beginner's mind there are many possibilities,
in the expert's mind there are few.
– Shunryu Suzuki

In the discussion on habits, I mentioned how a significant percentage of our decisions are rarely thought about. A disturbing corollary to that is that how we think and what we believe is also subject to the same shortcuts, called cognitive biases. In the next section, I will discuss how we observe processes, examine our current reality, and search for truth. Therefore, it is important to first understand and recognize how our experience, perspective, and bias can distort our observations.

One of the core concepts of Zen is *shoshin*, or "beginner's mind." This is a perspective that is free of preconceived ideas and opinions, and is open to new thought. I discussed earlier how some Lean concepts can be counterintuitive. Embracing shoshin requires "unlearning" what you thought you already knew—in effect, creating a beginner's mind. As we become older and supposedly wiser, creating a beginner's mind can become increasingly difficult. It becomes even more so when an entire team or organization needs to unlearn and develop a beginner's perspective.

Begin by focusing on questions, not answers. When observing a process, especially one you've seen many times, try to avoid jumping ahead to conclusions. Take one step (one question) at a time. Similarly, be aware that what seems like common sense may not be. Avoid using the word "should" as it implies a predetermined or expected outcome. Be careful with experience. What you already know should be an input, not a perspective. Be comfortable with saying "I don't know"—it shows a desire to learn and is a component of humility.

Being biased is a result of not having a beginner's mind. The most common and well-known bias is confirmation bias. This is our desire to believe what we want to believe, to the extent that we consciously or subconsciously distort or interpret information to fit our preconceptions. We can also seek out sources of information that align with our biases, while ignoring non-confirming data.

You can see an example of confirmation bias in the politics of the United States. It is the reason the two major parties in the U.S. are moving away from the center and more toward the extremes. Even though the number of information sources has exploded over the last couple decades, people on the right of the spectrum consume news geared toward them, because they feel it is correct. In other words, it fits their biases. The same happens on the left. This has occurred to such an extent that heroes of each party—Ronald Reagan and John F. Kennedy, for example—probably wouldn't be welcome in their parties today.

A second form of bias is loss aversion. Researchers such as psychologists Daniel Kahneman and Amos Tversky have found that we're twice as likely to try to avoid a loss than go after a gain. In effect, we are risk averse, which may be great for our survival as a species, but it hinders us as we try to create organizational change and improvement.

A third form of bias is conformity bias, also known as groupthink (e.g., "When in Rome..."). By nature, most of us don't like to stand out in a crowd and will be willing to agree with a group, even if we know the information is incorrect.

A fourth type is survivorship bias, where we focus on the tiny fraction of people that are successful, ignoring the far greater numbers that have failed. An example of this is our fascination with and attraction to get-rich-quick gurus. We also look at highly successful people like Steve Jobs and Bill Gates, and think that could be us. We then try to model ourselves after them. We find it easy to ignore, or not even understand, that every path is unique and what works for one person may not for another, for a multitude of reasons.

Finally—and this one is very common in the business world—is anchoring, or first impression bias. This form of bias occurs because we subconsciously give the first piece of information we receive on a topic more relevance and weight than follow-up information. This is why public relations companies find it very important to get their story out first, and why it is so difficult to change minds after the fact—even if the subsequent information is more accurate.

Once we know that we're susceptible to these biases, what can we do? The most important thing to do is to be mindful and present. Observe your thoughts and ask validating questions. Why do you think this way? What are the arguments against your opinion? Review the forms of bias and honestly try to determine if they might be in play. Taking steps to neutralize your biases will help you make smarter, more rational decisions. Observe like a beginner.

Observe the Now

You can observe a lot by just watching.
– Yogi Berra

Mindful observation takes effort and practice, but it is very valuable if you want to be a leader. It allows you to watch processes in action and look for small nuances and opportunities for improvement. For example, the wait staff at top-tier hotels do this every day. One waiter is always watching, looking for a shift in a customer's eyes that says she might need something, detecting a growing line of people waiting to be seated, or checking on food that needs to be delivered. This allows the staff to anticipate and resolve problems, often before the customers are aware they exist.

Being able to closely observe a situation allows things to flow much more smoothly.

The benefits of observation extend to the manufacturing setting as well. Taiichi Ohno had an exercise for his engineers and students where he'd draw a circle on the factory floor and tell them to stand in it and simply observe for a half hour. If they came back and reported that they didn't see anything to improve, he'd send them back out.

The Ohno Circle exercise is very powerful and can be used on the factory floor, in the finance department, or even at home with the kids. In fact, it's probably even more powerful in areas where processes are not visible or visibly defined. Just stand and watch. Resist the temptation to immediately jump into action. Think about and record what you've observed. Then improve it. In the Lean world, this is *genchi genbutsu*—go, see, and observe.

High-end hotels generally have observation down to a science. It is a core component of how they deliver great service. Several years ago, I was having a quiet breakfast at the Four Seasons in Bangkok after arriving late the previous evening. My table was at the side of an open atrium, so I was able to watch the staff in action. I've always been amazed by how the Four Seasons staff, whether at the restaurants or elsewhere, will be at your side exactly the instant you need them, but are also never annoyingly intrusive. Now I know how they do it.

Amidst the flurry of wait staff running around, I noticed there was always at least one person just standing and watching. It was not always the same person, but there was always one just looking around the room at the customers and the rest of the staff. If a customer looked up and around, indicating they needed something, the observing wait person immediately went over to that customer, while another staff member took over the watching and looking. If a line started to form at the front of the restaurant, the observer would head over and help with the seating. If another member of the wait staff needed help, he or she would have it within seconds and someone else would take over the watching. Someone was always standing, observing, and watching.

To test my own observation, I looked up and to the side, as if I needed something. Instantly, a waiter was at my side. I asked what he was watching for, and his response? "Just observing, sir." Yes, "just" observing. There was no "just" about it. Observation is a key to their exceptional customer service. I wanted to ask if process improvements were identified and acted on, but the language barrier between my server and me hindered our conversation.

When observing a process, be it on the factory floor or in the accounting office, it is important to mindfully observe without prejudice, staying in the present, without trying to identify solutions. Simply watch, look for details, and, when appropriate, document them.

Document the Current State

All truths are easy to understand once they are discovered;
the point is to discover them.
– Galileo Galilei

Before you can improve something, you must first have a very clear understanding of what its current state is. Don't assume you know what it is. Go to the gemba, be it the factory floor, the shipping and receiving area, your office, or even take a minute to focus on yourself, and observe what is going on. It is important that you get close to the action. The worst thing you can do is try to document the current state from a meeting in a faraway conference room.

To document key processes, such as accounts payable, production, sales, and so forth, document the current step-by-step activities of each of those processes. How long does each step take? How are they physically laid out? Where do backlogs occur?

If you are documenting the current state of a company or organization, there are a variety of ways to do it. You can use the key metrics of the organization, including financials, customer service, quality, operations, and so forth. If they are not the appropriate metrics, create new ones. Then decide how your observations compare to your expectations, industry average, etc. What are your suppliers saying about you? Your customers? Your employees? What about your competition?

Once you have your observations, you might want to consider using some standard analysis methods as well. These include a SWOT (strength, weakness, opportunity, threat) analysis, Porter's Five Forces (to analyze your industry), a PEST analysis (for the external macroenvironment), and BCG or GE methods to look at product lines.

From a Lean perspective, you may also want to look at how some key Lean tools are being used (5S, kaizen, poka-yoke, etc.). But remember, they are just tools. Moving forward, you need to determine if they are the right tools for the problem you are trying to solve. What is the problem or opportunity you want to address?

When documenting the current state, be sure to include other people with potentially other perspectives to validate the results. This will help you counteract your own biases. The current state becomes the baseline from which you will start improving. Finally, as I mentioned earlier, consider documenting the current state of you. What are you currently dealing with, your hopes, fears, and aspirations?

Envision the Future State

If you don't know where you are going, you'll end up someplace else.
– Yogi Berra

So now you have defined your principles, your *why?* (purpose), and your mission, and you've thoroughly analyzed the current state of your organization, process, or even you. It's time to look into the future. This is exciting as you get to dream and be creative!

Based on your *why?*, what would the ideal future state of your organization, process, or yourself look like? Think toward the long term, perhaps a very long term. What would happen if there were no constraints? What would your metrics be? What new business segments or technologies should you bring online to grow or to mitigate risk? What does your team and employees look like in terms of function and capability?

You could look at other organizations for ideas, but be very careful with benchmarking. Simply adopting someone else's best practice usually doesn't work. Every organization's context, perspective, goals, capabilities, and values are different.

Another way to look at a potential future state is to consider what perfection would look like. If your goal is perfection, then some other organization's best practice may seem like a mere stepping stone. Thinking about perfection as a possibility can radically change your perspective. Finally, once again, think about you. Where would you like to be—physically, mentally, spiritually, and emotionally—in ten or more years? Document this future state, just like you did for the current state.

Now compare the current and future state documents. Where are the gaps? What are the priorities of the gaps? Which are the most critical to your survival? Which have the most promise? Which are low hanging fruit that can be bridged quickly? Does the future state still align with your principles, why?, and mission? Do all of the stakeholders agree? After going through this process and answering these questions, you should have a defined future state document, showing prioritized gaps and opportunities.

Create the Hoshin Plan

A goal without a plan is just a wish.
- Antoine de Saint-Exupéry

Now that you have defined your future state and understand what gaps you need to bridge to get there, it's time to create a plan for action. In Lean, there is a form of strategic planning called *hoshin kanri*, also known as hoshin planning, or policy deployment. Hoshin means "set direction" and kanri means "together." With hoshin planning, you set a direction together with your team and organization, which is a bit different than a traditional strategic planning process.

The first step in creating a hoshin plan is to list the top three to five long-term or *ultimate goals* from your future state. Then, you and your team develop a set of intermediate-term (three to five years out) *breakthrough objectives*. Breakthrough objectives are very significant improvements or changes, and they should be linked to each of the long-term goals from above. Next, you develop a set of annual objectives for the next year that are tied to each of the breakthrough objectives. Keep SMART in mind for the objectives: you want them to be specific, measurable, attainable, realistic, and timely.

I once ran a very successful company that manufactured products based on a single material: silicone. Although we were the leaders in the industry and the properties of the material were very unique, we were always aware of the danger that a competitor could develop an alternate or improved material. In our hoshin plan, we had a long-term goal to be more diversified and protected from such a disruption. The related intermediate-term break-through objective was to have a specific but small (due to lengthy development timelines) percentage of our business use non-silicone materials. Our annual objectives were to first identify specific types of alternate materials that might fit with our technology and existing customer base, then determine whether that investment should come from an organic development or an acquisition, and then to start production.

Many leaders forget two critical components when planning: who will implement the objectives and how they will be implemented. Sometimes, a leader will assign the who and let that person decide how it will be done. It is critical to assign specific people to be responsible for each breakthrough and annual objectives and also to determine how the objectives will be accomplished. It is important to know in advance if there will be sufficient resources to accomplish all of the goals or if other activities may need to be reduced in priority.

The last step is to validate the hoshin plan with all stakeholders by performing what is known as *catchball*. Catchball is a process where the plan is circulated among the people who will be responsible for its implementation, prior to undertaking it. Stakeholders confirm that the plan is realistic and supports the principles and *why?* of the company, then offer suggestions for improvement if necessary. The output of catchball is a plan that everyone agrees on and has ownership in.

Short, But Not Too Short

It is my ambition to say in ten sentences
what others say in a whole book.
- Friedrich Nietzsche

Two decades ago, when I was in my first real executive role, I was asked to come up with a strategy for my business unit. For the first time in my career, I was in control and could develop and set my team's direction! I was excited to finally use some of what I had learned in my business school courses and seminars.

The team and I set to work, creating SWOTs, PESTs, Porter's Five Forces, and other analyses. We performed assessments, identified gaps, and finally, came up with our strategies. Then we developed plans for technology, markets, people and quality, with detailed action steps written out for each one. The whole exercise filled up a very nice-looking binder that we duplicated and presented to my management team. When we were done, we all looked in awe at what we had created. Then we proceeded to put it on a shelf—where it probably still sits today—and went back to the business of firefighting the company's day-to-day issues.

Why didn't our plan get used? For starters, it was too long, by a factor of twenty. Did we really think we would refer back to it on an ongoing basis? Just as what happens with traditional budgeting, the vast majority of the plan was obsolete within a couple months. Creating the multi-faceted self-analysis was valuable, but it was only valid for one point in time.

After seeing few benefits from our first strategy creation

process, you'd think I would have learned my lesson, but I didn't. I went through that same exercise a couple more times in different, larger, organizations. We created more pretty binders sitting on shelves. One of the last ones was even a hoshin-style plan, with long-term strategies tied to intermediate-term objectives that were tied to annual goals. The whole thing was just a long list of them.

And that was the problem: our desire for detail, specificity, depth, and breadth created too much complexity. At one of our quarterly reflection meetings, we realized that we weren't even using the plans we spent so much time creating, so we decided to change direction. We reduced our long-term strategies to three, wrote down a similar number of intermediate-term objectives, and tied them to about five annual goals. That was it for a fairly large, multi-site operation. We allowed our hoshin plan to evolve and change throughout the year as situations changed, similar to how some enlightened companies have dispensed with the annual budgeting process to use rolling and ongoing financial decision-making. We mapped all existing activities against that plan, and eliminated or delayed projects that weren't aligned. Once we simplified things, we began to achieve real forward progress. It was amazing how much time we freed up by getting rid of supposedly worthy projects that were not aligned with our strategy.

When I go into organizations as a consultant or simply as a visitor, I often see similar binders on the shelves, almost always gathering dust. I counsel the executives to create another plan, but this time, dramatically reduce its length and create an ongoing hansei (reflection) process. It seems to work much better.

Brevity is better when it comes to strategy. In 2014, Nick

Tasler wrote a piece for Harvard Business Review (HBR) titled *It's Time to Put Your Strategy on a Diet*, where he draws several parallels between strategic planning, eating, and dieting. In the article, Tasler writes that you should "limit your plate size" by reducing your number of priorities. Next, he advises readers to "let them eat cake…tomorrow" by putting off (but not forgetting about) great ideas that don't align with the current strategy. Then, he encourages us to avoid the "what-the-hell" effect (allowing one small deviation from the diet to lead to many others) through strict adherence to the strategy. Finally, Tasler writes, you should surround yourself with healthy eaters (others who understand the importance of limiting your projects and priorities) who are also skilled at leading.

While being concise is best, it is possible to take the idea too far. In *The Art of Crafting a 15-Word Strategy Statement* (also in HBR) Alessandro Di Fiore may take the concept of strategy brevity a little too much to the extreme when he suggests that only 15 words are necessary. Di Fiore's idea, although it could be a good exercise as part of the strategy development process, can lead you to create strategies so narrow that they are constraining, making them likely to end up forgotten on a wall in the corner of a conference room, next to the shelf holding a thick binder labeled Strategic Plan.

As you look up from reading this and notice your own binder on a shelf, think about taking another stab at it. Narrow it down. Be concise. What are the three or four long-term strategies that your organization needs to be focused on? What three or four measurable objectives must happen in the intermediate three- to five-year time frame for that to happen? What four or five projects must be accomplished this year to enable that? Finally, and perhaps most importantly, what is your organization working on right now that doesn't align with that plan? Stop doing it. Formally reflect on your strategic plan at least once a quarter with your team. Be prepared to adjust and evolve—don't just set it in stone once a year.

The One Big Thing

A true BHAG is clear and compelling, serves as unifying focal point of effort, and acts as a clear catalyst for team spirit. It has a clear finish line, so the organization can know when it has achieved the goal; people like to shoot for finish lines.
– James Collins and Jerry Porras

In their 1996 book, *Built to Last*, James Collins and Jerry Porras presented the concept of the Big Hairy Audacious Goal, or BHAG. A BHAG is a goal so bold and so transformative that the organization must radically change to achieve it. The leader's job is to emotionally galvanize the entire organization to support and work toward it, even if it could be decades away.

A BHAG is typically the result of a very serious threat or unusually lucrative opportunity. Collins and Porras identified four types of BHAGs, and give some examples:

- Target-oriented: Achieve a specific goal, such as Boeing's BHAG (before the term was coined) in 1950 to become the dominant player in commercial aviation.

137

- Competitive: Achieve a competitive goal, such as Nike's quest in the 1960s to "crush Adidas."
- Role Model: Obtain a position similar to one held by another company in another industry, such as Giro Sport Design's desire in 1986 to "become the Nike of cycling."
- Internal Transformation: Create a radical internal shift, such as Merck's 1930s effort to change from a chemical manufacturer into one of the world's largest pharmaceutical companies.

One purpose of a BHAG is to get the team to think big rather than focusing on smaller goals. Thinking big pushes people out of their comfort zone and forces them to look at alternatives and solutions they may not otherwise consider. Although BHAGs may have timeframes as long as a decade, they still create a sense of urgency that can galvanize and motivate an organization. The timeframe of a BHAG is also often longer than the expected tenure of the leader that created it, thereby creating enthusiasm and a stabilizing loyalty to the company rather than a person.

Do any of your long-term goals rise to the level of a BHAG? Would having one help focus your efforts in the right direction? One word of caution: a BHAG must stay consistent for many years. Otherwise, it loses its impact.

All On One Page

The single biggest problem in communication
is the illusion that it has taken place.
- George Bernard Shaw

It is important to effectively communicate and regularly update any plan that guides an organization. Several decades ago, Toyota pioneered what is now known in the Lean world as *A3 Thinking*, where the company's entire plan is shown and updated on one sheet of paper. (A3 is a standard size of the paper, roughly the same as 11" x 17" in the United States.)

There are four general categories of A3s:
- Problem-solving
- Proposal
- Status report
- Strategic planning

All four follow the same general approach of embedding Plan-Do-Check-Act (PDCA) thinking. Each has a section that compares where you are versus where you want to be that includes clear metrics, a section showing the steps (and status) to accomplish the plan, and a section to check for effectiveness

The A3 does not have a defined format as long as the core components are used. However, it is often beneficial to standardize formats within an organization to improve the efficiency of review. A higher-level A3, such as an A3 containing an organization's hoshin plan for strategy, will typically spawn lower-level A3s to show specific annual goals and other projects. Some examples of A3s are in the Appendix.

Although it may seem tedious to create an A3 for each project or strategy, the act of creating it generates learning and understanding in itself—one reason the concept is called A3 Thinking. Then, when used as part of a regular review process and posted in a visible area, the A3 becomes a great tool for communication and ongoing project discipline and accountability. I'll discuss A3s more in the section on execution.

Part Six - Simplify

That's been one of my mantras—focus and simplicity. Simple can be harder than complex: You have to work hard to get your thinking clean to make it simple. But it's worth it in the end because once you get there, you can move mountains.

– Steve Jobs

After you have clarified your plans, one of the best things you can do as you implement them is to simplify them as much as possible. Although many activities to simplify your personal and professional life seem obvious, they should still be performed within a context of your clear plan. This will help you choose the correct actions for reaching your goals in the most efficient manner.

Key Points from this Section:
- Simplify your work area and life by ensuring that every item has value, and then has a place. Strive to minimize.
- Ensure all projects and activities support your principles, *why?*, mission, and hoshin plan.
- Remove choice and be comfortable saying "no" respectfully.
- Organize your workspace so that it communicates information visually. Visual information is processed far faster than written.
- Write by hand to improve learning.

Declutter and Organize

The ability to simplify means to eliminate the unnecessary so that
the necessary may speak.
– Hans Hofman

Look around your office, your factory, and your home. What do you see? Do you really need all of that stuff on your desk and shelves? Is there a purpose to each item? Does it need to be available now, or can it be put out of sight for a few weeks, months, or even forever? How much time do you consume (and stress do you create) by looking for the appropriate tool, book, or utensil? Does your kitchen really need three beat-up measuring cups of the same size? How much does it cost to maintain and clean all of your extra stuff? What does the space, additional complexity, and distraction cost?

Over time, things in our lives (and our companies) accumulate, and we end up wasting a lot time and effort managing them. To reduce the cost of unnecessary stuff, we use a core tool of Lean called 5S. The term 5S comes from five Japanese words that roughly translate to sort, straighten, shine, standardize, and sustain:

- *Sort:* Review each item, ensure it has a purpose, remove what isn't needed.
- *Straighten*: Find a defined location for what remains, preferably as close to where it will be used as possible.
- *Shine:* Clean and polish the newly uncluttered area.
- *Standardize*: Create a checklist or other method to ensure the

area doesn't revert back to how it was.

- *Sustain:* Create a habit, routine, or daily activity to keep the area clean and neat, and to audit that it has stayed that way.

In short, you remove what isn't needed, find a defined home for what remains, clean up your space, turn the activity into a habit, and find a way to ensure it continues. Using 5S ensures that your factory floor has only the tools that are needed, in just the right place, and are always returned to that place.

On the best factory floors, and in the best restaurant kitchens, you will often find shadow boards where every required tool is hung on a wall with the outline of the utensil tool behind it. Everyone knows where to go to get the tool—there are no extra tools that need to be sorted through to find the right one. It is visually obvious when a tool is missing.

Decluttering also has a Zen component. I encourage you to find one room, or even one shelf, and evaluate the objects you see. Challenge each one. Why is it there, and what is its purpose? What would happen if it wasn't there? If it has a reason and has real value, then find and define a home for it.

Cleaning can become obsessive, so be sure the effort adds value and aligns with your principles. Does marking the location of your phone on your desk truly add value? Probably not. However, having a clean, neat environment will help give you the focus and strength to tackle more important challenges. Once you have your workspace in order, you will soon realize that simplifying and uncluttering doesn't just apply to physical stuff.

To be most effective, the cleaning needs to be targeted,

not indiscriminately applied. The same boss I described earlier, who asked his employees whether they were "incompetent or just incapable," also had a painful (for us) Friday afternoon cleaning routine. Around three or four o'clock, he would take a look at his desktop, decide that any paperwork on it he hadn't already looked at must not be important, and sweep everything into the trash can. This was three decades ago, when most reports were still typed on typewriters, so recreating them was difficult. His staff soon developed a routine of going to his office around two in the afternoon to retrieve any unread reports and paperwork from his desk, just to redeposit them there on Monday morning.

Understanding value is critical before tackling a decluttering project.

Minimize

Perfection is achieved, not when there is nothing more to add,
but when there is nothing left to take away.
– Antoine de Saint-Exupery

If you've removed the clutter in your life, then the last thing you really want to do is add something. Or so you'd think. Unfortunately, our culture has conditioned us to always want more. We like our toys. We buy impulsively. We take on too many projects. (Well, at least I used to.)

Zen teaches us the value of *koko*, or austerity. This doesn't mean you have to live the life of a monk, having no real possessions and relying on the morning alms for nutrition, but it does mean challenging yourself to find the point where you have what you need and nothing more. That point is different for each of us, and an item or expense that is a toy or luxury to one person may be a valuable component of another's life. The purpose is to become consciously aware, and to make a conscious decision before adding something new.

Most of us have seen the famous photo of Steve Jobs sitting in the middle of his living room on a mat, sipping tea, surrounded by just a single lamp and a couple of books. Living so frugally is probably not how most of us would choose to live, but consider the freedom—and focus—that lifestyle creates (not to mention the fatter savings account, which in itself creates more freedom).

You should have seen the look on my real estate agent's face years ago when I told her I wanted a house with less storage space and not more. It was obviously the first time she had heard that request, especially from someone looking for a nicer house. After looking at several options that did not fit our vision of a nicer but smaller house, my wife and I decided to build our own. The project has created many new minimization ideas, and our architect is working on a design that minimizes doors and walls, reduces angles and unnecessary trim, and lowers the number of horizontal surfaces upon which clutter can be stacked. All these features will help us reduce our lives' clutter and avoid the temptation to buy more things.

145

The Waste of Choice

Owning fewer keys opens more doors.
– Alex Morritt

An abundance of choices and the decisions that accompany them are both a benefit and curse of the modern world. Each decision we make, no matter how small, uses up a little bit of the mental energy we have available every day. By focusing on reducing our options and minimizing the number of choices we must make, life becomes simpler and calmer.

David Cain recently wrote a great piece on his Raptitude blog on decision-making and minimalism called *Why the Minimalists Do what They Do*. As an aspiring minimalist, the topic appealed to me, and Cain's commentary on choice and decisions was especially apropos.

I've been lucky in that I've always had an ability to make good decisions quickly, regardless of whether I base them on real analysis or just wing it from the gut. (Yes, intuitive decisions can still be good.) This skill has been invaluable in my career and my personal life. However, most people I know are less fortunate, and I've noticed how indecision impacts many aspects of their lives. From professional decisions such as what path to take with a new product development project, to personal decisions such as where to go for dinner, not being able to make a decision creates stress for both the person making the decision and those being impacted by the decision.

The problem is compounded with age. For example, in a

146

relative's last years, I watched her become literally debilitated and frozen by even the most basic decisions. Because she couldn't make decisions, the number of undecided issues made her life appear to be unnecessarily and impossibly complex.

To combat our indecision, we need to simplify our lives. Cain describes how he eats the same thing for breakfast every morning. By doing so, he removes a couple of decisions from his day, allowing him to focus better on other things. I can relate. My breakfast is the same cup of Greek yogurt and Grape Nuts each morning. I eat it while reading *The Wall Street Journal* on my iPad, just after my morning meditation and stretching, and just before reviewing my journal and starting my Hour of Power. I do this every day. The routine is satisfying, and calming.

The implications of reducing our number of choices go far beyond our daily meals. Simple is clearer, and fewer options tax the brain less. For example, the best websites intuitively guide you among very few choices. Well-planned standard work reduces the variation of subjectivity while providing a foundation for kaizen. In other words, when workers don't have to make unnecessary decisions, they have the mental energy to explore better ways to perform their tasks.

Where can you reduce options in your life and in your organization, thereby reducing the waste and unnecessary complexity of indecision, and the variability of multiple decisions?

Align and Eliminate

My success, part of it certainly,
is that I have focused in on a few things.
– Bill Gates

Once you have a hoshin plan detailing what your organization's priorities are, it's time to face the reality of all the other projects you and your group are currently working on. This is often a "come-to-Jesus" time when organizational politics can reach a fever pitch, as project owners pitch why their projects, perhaps their raison d'être, deserve survival. It is also a great time to demonstrate the power of the hoshin plan as well as your leadership commitment to a new, defined path forward.

Compile a list of all current projects and significant activities. (This in itself will probably be an eye-opening experience.) Then, as a team, map that list against your principles, mission, *why?*, and hoshin plan. The hoshin plan will not list all the company's appropriate or valuable projects, but it should contain the highest-priority objectives. All other projects must align to the principles, *why?*, and mission, and support and not conflict with the plan.

Project managers and teams on projects that no longer align with the organization's future path should not be fearful. If done correctly, the projects on the hoshin plan will stretch the organization and need experienced project managers and teams to work on them. Think about how much easier your leadership role will be when all projects are identified and aligned with a hoshin plan that the organization owns and supports, not to mention the resources that are being saved or better invested.

Once again, consider doing the same for you personally. What are you working on that isn't giving you value or contributing to your own plan? Eliminating the nonessentials in your life will give you more time and focus to create something you want even more.

Just Say No

Clarity about what is essential fuels us with the strength
to say no to the nonessentials.
– Greg McKeown

Two years ago, while on my end-of-year reflection trip, I read Greg McKeown's *Essentialism*. What a great book! In it, McKeown discusses how to identify your essential projects, activities, and belongings, so that you can then identify (and eliminate) the nonessential ones.

Once you know what is not necessary, you figure out how to get rid of it. Similar to how we eliminated projects that didn't align with our hoshin plan, we need to get rid of activities and things that are not essential to implement it. One of McKeown's admonitions is "if it isn't a 'hell yes' then it's a 'hell no.'"

I was able to convince several people at my current company to read Essentialism, so we've used that last statement on many occasions. When interviewing candidates for a position, we ask ourselves if he or she is a "hell yes." If we don't have that level of enthusiasm, then it's back to the applicant pool. The same goes for potential partnerships, new projects, and equipment. Yes, it's somewhat subjective, and we do use more quantitative analyses when appropriate, but that last gut call is valuable.

Another key revelation from the book was on how to say no to requests in a way that conveys your time is valuable. If you explain the reasons why you cannot help someone and do so in an authentic manner, requestors will get over their disappointment and you will still have their respect. Perhaps the hardest thing to do, but something that can really improve productivity, is to say "no" to things we want to do—even to good and valuable projects and activities. This forces us to prioritize, thereby focusing our time, resources, and attention on what really matters.

I have used this concept with considerable success over the past year. I've turned down speaking engagements I wasn't interested in, collaborations that I didn't think would go anywhere (in the past, I might have tried anyway), and meetings where I was invited but didn't really need to be there. This has freed up a lot of my time and reduced the stress and drudgery of having to do things that didn't add value, allowing me to invest my limited time more wisely. Sure, I still use a lot of my time to help others, but I now do it more methodically (and, in my opinion, better and more mindfully).

Reduce Information Overload

*Everybody gets so much information all day long
that they lose their common sense.*
– Gertrude Stein

Information overload is a big problem in modern society. We only have so much time and mental capacity to process information, and if we are not careful, the abundance can overwhelm us. We need to make it a priority to wisely manage the information-sharing systems at our companies, including email, phone calls, and voicemail.

Emails can be a big productivity killer if not managed properly. How many emails are in your inbox right now? If you're like most people, you have dozens, perhaps hundreds. I know a couple folks who have over a thousand! What good is that? Having so many emails in your inbox will make you feel overwhelmed just by looking at it. How is that respecting yourself?

I used to have more than a couple hundred emails in my inbox at any one time. When it got to be too many, I'd re-sort the inbox by sender and mass delete emails from people I considered to be a lower priority than others. Yes, I really did that. I was not exactly showing respect for people, let alone being mindful of the problems it could create for them and the organization.

This changed for me when a few years ago I came across a blog post touting "Inbox: Zero." My reaction was, really? Zero emails in your inbox? Although I was skeptical, I gave it a try and haven't looked back since. I can't remember the last time I had more than ten emails in my inbox, and I try to get to zero by each evening.

To stay near or at Inbox: Zero takes effort and discipline, which needs to turn into habit. These are the steps to do it:

1. Aggressively unsubscribe from newsletters and promotional emails, unless you are willing to read them within one day. With the ones that remain, move them to a "To Read" folder immediately, or send them there automatically via an email rule.
2. Aggressively remove yourself from group distribution lists that are not critical.
3. If you were just cc'd or bcc'd on an email, scan quickly and make every attempt to not reply, then delete. Ask the sender to remove you from the chain if your attention isn't critical to the matter.
4. Add (or decline) invitations to your calendar immediately. Be aggressive about declining if you don't believe the meeting adds value—remember the Just Say No section above.
5. Try to take action (or respond) to an email immediately whenever possible. Otherwise, move it to a "To-Do" folder. I've now become good enough at this that my inbox is my residual to-do folder, generally with less than five tasks to be completed. Many people say this is the worst use for an inbox, but with so few emails it works well.

I can't describe how liberating this process is. Now, I can give far better attention to the few remaining emails I have and generate more thoughtful and focused responses while respecting the senders and their issues.

Beyond cleaning up your own inbox, you can also help create a better email culture within your organization. First, be very judicious about who is copied on emails, and insist others respect your time as well. An "FYI," if truly needed in the first place, does not need to be sent to a broad audience—that's generally more a "CYA" (cover your you-know-what). Second, insist that any desired action be very clearly stated in an email, right at the top. Third, be very concise with original and reply emails. I had a big problem with this, and was known as the king of the long-winded email. I continue to struggle with being too wordy, and have a goal to try to keep emails to three sentences or less.

There are other aspects to email management that help increase your productivity. For example, I try to only check email four times a day, keeping in line with the pomodoro method I described earlier. I hope to reduce that to three times next year. I turned off auto-checking on my phone so I don't get disturbed with each new email. I also aggressively clear out old saved emails. They may not technically cost anything, and they are searchable history, but they still seem like clutter. I am now actually very close to not only Inbox: Zero, but also Mailbox: Zero!

While email is a known productivity killer, phone and voicemail can also create information overload, if not managed properly. I have never been a fan of using the phone, even though I know it is often a more effective and immediate communication tool than email. I prefer to receive an email so I can properly contemplate and formulate a response. Many organizations, such as Coca-Cola, are turning off their voicemail systems to push people to use email or live phone conversations.

Because of this, and because people know I'm not very good at responding to phone calls, I more regularly use voicemails. (If I did, I'd probably manage very similarly to my email inbox: aggressively filter, and respond immediately.) One thing about the voicemail system that I do love is that any incoming voicemails are also sent to my email inbox. There's even a service that will auto-transcribe them into the email, so I don't have to listen to the audio (plus, they are searchable). I know several people that like sending audio messages via email, but in my opinion, they are wasteful for the receiver, as they cannot be quickly scanned and searched. My friend Paul Akers uses them very effectively, but I know others that take two minutes to convey ten seconds of information—which isn't respecting my time.

Regardless of how you accomplish it, reducing your information overload is very important if you want to be an effective leader. By taking steps to slim down the amount of information that reaches you, you will be able to be more effective with the tasks that truly need your time and attention.

Go Visual

Make your workplace into showcase that can be understood by everyone at a glance.
– Taiichi Ohno

We've all heard the phrase that a picture is worth a thousand words. There's actually a scientific rationale for that: the brain processes visual information 60,000 times faster than written information. Almost half of the nerve fibers in the brain are linked to the retina and ninety percent of the information processed by the brain is visual. As such, when running an organization, it makes much more sense to visit the gemba and see what is happening there than to sit in an office reading reports about it.

Two core concepts of Lean are removing waste and showing respect for people. Managing your workplace more visually helps with both. By making information visual and public, you convey information more quickly and efficiently. You also show respect for people by clearly communicating the status and expectations of the organization to them. With effective visual management, all employees can align their actions to the goals of the organization.

As Taiichi Ohno said (see quote above), the goal of visual management is to convey the status of the organization at a glance. This can be done in various ways, including posting A3 reports on strategies and projects, metrics boards, production schedule boards, shadow boards for tools, kamishibai boards, and kanban. In Lean operations, you will see andons, which are visual status indicators such as red/green lights on machines, and there will often be markings on the floor to indicate the correct location of equipment and supplies. Many Lean organizations also have an obeya, a single room that has the key visual management and control charts for the organization. (Note: the obeya is not a "war room!") To respect people, it should be open and accessible to as many employees as possible. In my last company, a wide section of the main hallway effectively served as an obeya, The hallway was also where we held our daily executive standup meeting. The meeting, and the information on the wall, were open to everyone, so that anyone passing through the hall could quickly check the status of the company without having to sit down and read through a long report. This allowed us to leverage the capacity of the human brain to process visual information, reduce waste, and show more respect for our employees.

Learning by Writing by Hand

Writing, to me, is simply thinking through my fingers.
– Isaac Asimov

I'm an early-adopter tech geek at heart, and am generally among the first to embrace a new technology. I may not go to the extreme of standing in line for a new iPhone, but I will pay to upgrade to the latest model, even when I have difficulty describing the changes compared to the previous model. I even owned an Apple Newton for a while. (Remember that summer of 1993? Probably not.)

Not every technology I use is the most recent, however. I love my gizmos, but there's one area where I'm still decidedly old school. I prefer to write by hand, because I believe I learn better through writing than typing.

The psychology behind the learning advantage of handwriting is starting to be understood. A study by Pam Mueller and Daniel Oppenheimer, published in *Psychological Science*, found that college students who handwrote their notes remembered conceptual information better immediately after the class than those who took notes on a computer. A week later, the note takers remembered both factual and conceptual information better.

This is why I regularly harp on the advantages of writing on whiteboards over typing into a computer and then converting the data into reports or electronic displays. When you write a production number, metric, or problem on a whiteboard, you own that number, you visually see the relationship between it and the numbers next to it, and you recognize patterns and trends more easily.

Typing is much less personal. When you enter data into a computer, the data is transformed into other numbers and analyses that you may see a week or even month later, after the linkage, understanding, and ownership of that data has been lost. You end up with one group of people trained to feed the machine and a different group of people trained to supposedly interpret what the machine spits out.

Yes, writing by hand has its downsides. Handwriting is hard to search, repurpose, share, and archive. Whiteboards can be difficult to use across multiple sites and complex operations. That said, I wish I had a dime for every process I've seen that supposedly required a high-powered MRP system, when a whiteboard was more than sufficient.

Write things out, don't type them. You might be surprised with what happens. The process of writing by hand creates understanding, ownership, reflection, and thus learning that you might otherwise not have gained.

Part Seven – Improve

Plans are only good intentions unless they immediately degenerate into hard work. – Peter Drucker

After you clarify the principles and the *why?*, and create a hoshin plan, it's time to do something. To create improvement.

Key Points from this Section:

- Improvement activities, whether on an organization or a small process, should follow the PDSA (Plan-Do-Study-Adjust) cycle.
- Kaizen is the process of creating many improvements, by individuals or teams.
- Other improvement tools include value stream mapping, standard work, and improvement kata.
- Daily management and accountability are required to drive and sustain improvement.
- A key component of improvement is a practice of individual or team reflection.
- Celebrate success and learn from failure.

159

Start. Now.

The secret to getting ahead is getting started.
– Mark Twain

Getting started on a new project is tough. If you're trying to transform an entire organization, it can be even tougher because it requires you to make some changes. Changing yourself is often the toughest part—especially if it involves losing weight or modifying a habit. So what do you do?

The secret is to just start, and to do it now. You've already clarified why and how you need to change. You just need to do it.

This is easier said than done, as most of us are experts at coming up with reasons to procrastinate. We give ourselves excuses to avoid dealing with unacceptable behaviors or situations until the "right" time (e.g., the start of a new year) arrives. If our behavior is truly unacceptable, how can it be okay to wait to change it?

Another way we like to procrastinate is to form teams and make sure every detail is in place before we start anything new. This is folly. Your team is ready, with you as their leader. It is impossible to plan for everything that could possibly go wrong before you start a project. What are you really waiting for? How does delaying look to your team? Is it authentic? Is it respectful?

Last year, as soon as I learned how Paul Akers lost over fifty pounds, I was motivated to lose weight myself. If he could, I could—especially since I only needed to lose half that. Instead of waiting until the new year to change my eating habits I began at that very moment. Five minutes after reading his email describing what he had done, I went to Starbucks to get my usual vanilla latte. Instead, taking a cue from Paul, I bought a regular coffee and skipped the latte. That was the beginning of my health improvement journey. Ten weeks later, I was fifteen pounds lighter. (Coincidentally, the end of ten weeks happened to coincide with the new year, when I would have typically started pursuing a new goal.)

Don't wait. Start. Now.

Plan, Do, Study, Adjust

Excellent firms don't believe in excellence—
only in constant improvement and constant change.
– Tom Peters

The PDSA (Plan-Do-Study-Act) cycle is the core component of continuous improvement programs. You may have heard it called PDCA (Plan-Do-Check-Act)—and they are very similar— but I have come to prefer PDSA, with the A standing for Adjust, for reasons I'll explain shortly. Understanding the cycle and its application to continuous improvement is critical for leadership. But first, a history lesson.

In November 2010, Ronald Moen and Clifford Norman wrote a well-researched article in *Quality Progress* that detailed the history behind PDCA and PDSA. The cycles have their origins in 1939, when Walter Shewhart created the SPI (Specification-Production-Inspection) cycle. The SPI cycle was geared toward mass production operations, but Shewhart soon realized the potential application of the scientific method to problem solving,

161

writing that "it may be helpful to think of the three steps in the mass production process as steps in the scientific method. In this sense, specification, production and inspection correspond respectively to hypothesizing, carrying out an experiment and testing the hypothesis. The three steps constitute a dynamic scientific process of acquiring knowledge."

At the time, W. Edwards Deming was working with Shewhart to edit a series of Shewhart's lectures into what would become Shewhart's *Statistical Method from the Viewpoint of Quality Control*, published in 1939. Deming eventually modified the cycle and presented his DPSR (Design-Production-Sales-Research) cycle in 1950, which is now referred to as the Deming cycle or Deming wheel. According to Masaaki Imai, Toyota then modified the Deming wheel into the PDCA (Plan-Do-Check-Act) cycle and began applying it to problem solving.

In 1986, Deming again revised the Shewhart cycle, with another modification added in 1993 to make it the PDSA (Plan-Do-Study-Act) cycle, or what Deming called the Shewhart cycle for learning and improvement. (Deming never did like the PDCA cycle. In 1990, he wrote Ronald Moen, saying "be sure to call it PDSA, not the corruption PDCA." A year later he wrote, "I don't know the source of the cycle that you propose.

162

How the PDCA ever came into existence I know not.")

The PDCA cycle has not really evolved in the past 40 years and is still used today at Toyota. The PDSA cycle continues to evolve, primarily in the questions asked at each stage. Although both embody the scientific method, I personally prefer the PDSA cycle, because "study" is more intuitive than "check." Deming himself had a problem with the term "check," as he believed it could be misconstrued as "hold back." I also prefer "Adjust" to "Act," as it conveys a better sense of ongoing, incremental improvement. Just be aware that some very knowledgeable and experienced people prefer the pure PDCA!

Let's take a look at each component of PDSA:

- **Plan:** Ask objective questions about the process and create a plan to carry out the experiment: who, what, when, where, and a prediction.
- **Do:** Execute the plan, make observations, and document problems and unexpected issues.
- **Study:** Analyze the data, compare it to expectations, and summarize what was learned.
- **Adjust:** Adopt and standardize the new method if successful; otherwise, identify changes to be made in preparation for starting the whole cycle over again.

It's important to realize that PDSA cycle is valuable at both process and organizational levels, something we have already discussed (in slightly different terms) in this book. For example, you start the plan stage of the PDSA cycle while evaluating your current state and creating a hoshin plan. As you execute the annual and breakthrough objectives of the hoshin plan, you move into the "do" quadrant. On a regular basis, you evaluate the hoshin plan and the results of the goals (study), then modify it as necessary for the next revision of the hoshin plan (act).

Throughout the rest of this section, I will discuss various problem-solving and improvement tools and methods for process-scale improvements. Note that they all follow the same PDSA cycle.

Change for the Better

There are no big problems, just a lot of little problems.
– Henry Ford

Kaizen is probably the most important concept in the Toyota Production System. The word kaizen can be broken into its two components: kai, meaning "change," and zen, meaning "good." It was brought to the West in 1986, when Masaaki Imai wrote *Kaizen: The Key to Japan's Success*. I agree with Imai and others such as Bob Emiliani that say "there can be no Lean without kaizen."

Although kaizen is generally thought of as large numbers of small improvements that add up to create a large overall change, it is important to understand that this is not a restriction. Kaizen can be small activities by individuals, small ongoing team-based activities, focused multiple-day events to make rapid, significant improvements, or large improvement projects driven by executive staff.

In most companies, problem solving and improvement starts by having a team of managers carve an hour or two a week out of their schedules. Over several weeks, they discuss problems, typically in a conference room. They brainstorm ideas for changes or improvements and make detailed plans about how to implement their ideas. This process takes a lot of time, and may or may not actually solve any problems.

With kaizen, less time is spent planning and more time is spent experimenting. The planning takes place at the gemba, typically by the people directly involved in the process. These people have a better understanding of what is actually happening on the floor and are more likely to take ownership in the improvement process when they are included in the kaizen. Each individual experiment is relatively small, so there is a low risk that any one change will cause large negative impacts. Over time, the changes, especially the learning from continually planning, doing, studying, and revising, create large cumulative positive effects.

In addition to the individual or small-team kaizen activity with small experiments, Lean organizations also utilize *kaizen events* in order to aim for more radical changes. The events are generally three to five days long, with the entire team fully dedicated to the activity. During a kaizen event, the first day is spent planning, the next couple days are spent doing, and the final days are spent studying and acting on the results. Kaizen events can create very significant improvement in a short period of time. They are especially effective when someone from the senior leadership team helps facilitate the event, allowing approvals to purchase equipment or modify processes to be expedited.

Kaizen and kaizen events follow the PDSA cycle we previously discussed. The steps are:

1. Define the problem. (Plan)
2. Document the current state. (Plan)
3. Determine the desired future state with measurable targets. (Plan)
4. Identify solutions or improvements. (Plan)
5. Develop the plan. (Plan)
6. Implement the plan. (Do)
7. Study the results and compare to the plan, targets, and desired future state. (Study)
8. Document the change in standard work, or use what was learned to create the next experiment. (Adjust)
9. Document and publicize the kaizen activity. (Adjust)

The last step—documenting and publicizing the kaizen activity—is important and should not be neglected. Many Lean organizations have kaizen boards, kaizen newspapers, or kaizen "wall of fame" areas where such activities are made visible. This is both motivating to others and can inspire other ideas for improvement.

Another critical concept of kaizen, often missed by even the best Lean organizations, is "unlearning." Chihiro Nakao said, "You have to go back to zero. Put yourself under dire circumstances to think differently." Many business writers have discussed the "learning organization," but unlearning old standards, methods, or even rationales is just as important, if not more. Learn, and unlearn. Remember the Zen concept of beginner's mind?

The role of the leader in kaizen is critical. You must demonstrate and explain why kaizen is important for your organization. You should lead by example and personally lead both big and small kaizen. Ask your employees to participate in kaizen activity and support it by providing time, training, and mentoring. What a great way to get to know the folks at the gemba, and also to teach them about PDSA and improvement methods! Ask your leadership team to do the same. When you implement kaizen, be careful about creating arbitrary goals for the number of kaizen activities; instead, create a culture where kaizen is supported. Finally, celebrate kaizen, especially when learning occurs from failure. Learning is an improvement in itself.

When using kaizen, it is important to not sacrifice time for perfection. Remember, the goal is to create ongoing incremental improvements, not to find the perfect one-time solution.

The Human Side of Change

People don't resist change, they resist being changed.
– Peter Senge

To survive, an organization must be continually improving and changing. This requires both leadership commitment and the support and input from all employees. It is important to be mindful and aware of the concerns of everyone involved, in order to leverage their support.

As Peter Scholtes, author of *The Leader's Handbook*, noted

(see above), people don't automatically resist change. But they do want to understand the change and be given the opportunity to provide input, which creates ownership. This is one of the key advantages of kaizen: the change process includes people from all levels of the organization, particularly those that are part of the production process. Additionally, involving people in the kaizen efforts and giving people the training and support they need to create change shows respect for them.

Employees want to understand the impact of change on their livelihoods. Leaders can forget what it is like to live from paycheck to paycheck, and when people are fearful of how they will support their families, they tend to have a very conservative perspective on change. This will slow down the improvement process, unless leaders give workers transparency, trust, and ownership.

To create security, some Lean organizations tell their employees that no one will lose their jobs as a result of improvement activities. This is powerful, but you also want to be careful. Be sure to link the security directly to the improvement activities and avoid giving the impression that it transcends issues outside of your control, such as sudden changes in the market. You want to create trust, and trust requires transparency and only making promises you can keep.

To optimize improvement efforts, respect your people by asking them to play a key role in the improvement process. Give them confidence they will not be harmed by potential side effects of the improvement effort, offer training and mentoring so they know how to create improvements, and provide them with the time to identify and execute improvement activities. If you do these things, you will find they are more likely to embrace the changes you want.

Go and See

When you are out observing on the gemba, do something to help them. If you do, people will come to expect that you can help them and will look forward to seeing you again on the gemba.
– Taiichi Ohno

I briefly introduced you to the concept of the gemba earlier in this book. The definition of gemba is "the real place" or "where value is created," i.e., the production floor in a manufacturing company or a surgical ward in a hospital, and so forth.

Traditional business gurus talk about MBWA: management by walking around. What is that, really? Wandering around for what reason? What does that accomplish, besides perhaps provoking some fear?

Walking the gemba is different. You go to where value is being created and do more than just walk. You observe the process and ask questions, such as: What is the ideal state? What is the standard? Is there a problem? What is causing the gap between the ideal and the current state? You also check with the area manager to see if she sees the same things you do. Respect your team by helping them see the gemba the way you do, and listen to them describe what they see.

Use the gemba walk as a daily method to observe the

169

process, identify areas for improvement, support kaizen, and mentor others. During problem solving, your leadership team should be at the gemba observing the problem, not in a conference room discussing it.

In many Lean organizations, you will also see managers, executives—even presidents—with their desks at the gemba so they can observe it throughout the day. When my own team decided to put our offices on the second floor of a new building, we faced some potential downsides by being away from where the work was being done. However, our production operators and supervisors were developing rapidly and becoming independent and confident in their capabilities, so we felt that if we put our executive team on the shop floor, we would stymie that growth, which wouldn't be respecting people.

On the other hand, consider what I witnessed at the Sheraton Hongqiao in Shanghai a few years ago. As I walked into the bustling lobby of this large hotel, a man was working at a desk on the side. It was Thomas Mueller, the hotel's general manager. Mueller would work from that desk most of the day, able to directly observe the key gemba of his operation. Despite being very busy, he welcomed questions from guests, and if he had to leave for a few minutes, his assistant took over. Working in a bustling lobby probably wasn't the most productive location, but for him it was the most valuable one.

If you want to find out what is truly going on at your company, get out of the office or conference room and go and see what is happening where value is being created. Find the gemba and actively observe it, then look for ways to improve the work taking place there.

Standard Work

Where there is no standard, there can be no kaizen.
– Taiichi Ohno

Before you can create change, you must know exactly what you're currently doing. Beware—it's probably different than what you think it is! Earlier, in the Clarify section, I encouraged you to detail the current state of your organization. Now it's time to drill down and do the same for individual processes. There are two ways of doing this in a Lean organization, and they should be used together: The first is standard work, and the second is value stream

171

mapping, which I'll cover in the next section.

Standard work can and should be used for all types of processes—manufacturing, office, and even leadership activities. People and organizations are sometimes leery of implementing standard work because they believe it could hinder flexibility, but in reality, standard work enables change by documenting the current state. Once the current state is deeply understood by employees, they can look for ways to improve it.

At its most basic level, standard work is the documented sequence of operations in a process. In most cases, though, people implementing standard work incorporate additional information. The three components of standard work are:

- The *sequence* of steps in the process
- The *takt time* of the process, which is the rate the process needs to operate at to satisfy (but not exceed!) customer demand.
- The *inventory* necessary overall and at each step required for the process to operate at the defined takt time.

Companies use a variety of forms to implement standard work, including those that show the physical layout of the process (including machines, equipment, supplies, and workstations), as well as sheets that document the time required by steps in the process. Sometimes they use a combination sheet that includes both. These forms become part of the visual management of the process and are usually posted at the process location.

Leaders can use a form of standard work called leader standard work. Similar to process standard work, leader standard work defines the activities an individual leader performs as part of his or her responsibilities. The type of leader standard work varies considerably, depending on the level and responsibility of the position.

For example, production cell leaders may spend only part of their day on leadership activities, spending the remainder of their time actually working in the production process. Others may spend the majority of their time performing tasks on their leader standard work sheet. They may audit the 5S and workplace organization of the cell each morning and each evening, review order flow, review quality issues, and ensure appropriate staffing is planned, etc.

A senior executive may have a leader standard work sheet that is completely different. On a daily basis, the executive may review operating and quality statistics from the previous day, lead the daily standup meeting, review the leader standard work sheets of other leaders, and do a gemba walk. Other activities, such as reviewing customer information, providing feedback to team members, leading a kaizen event, providing information to other executives, ensuring alignment to the hoshin plan, and so forth, may happen on a weekly, monthly, quarterly, or even annual basis.

The key point is that these leadership activities are listed and standardized, and completion is documented each day. The completed leader standard work sheets are often posted in a common area or near the leader's work area as part of visual management.

Similarly, standard work and leader standard work can be

173

used on a personal level. You could have standard work for how to close down your house before leaving for an extended period of time, how to prepare for winter, and what to do in case of an emergency. You could create leader standard work to ensure you review financial accounts, plan meals and check the pantry, perform regular maintenance on your car, or replace furnace filters.

More information on standard work and leader standard work, including forms and examples, are in the Resources section.

Map the Value Stream

One of the most powerful Lean tools is called value stream mapping, a visual management method used to document the flow and creation of value in a process. The definition of a value stream is all steps—value-added and non-value-added—that contribute to taking the process from raw materials (or raw data, etc.) to the customer. As with the other tools I've discussed, value stream mapping can be used to understand and document the production floor, in-office processes, hospital surgical wards, and, once again, even at home.

The first step in value stream mapping is to choose the process you want to improve, which will then be mapped. I recommend starting with a small, easily-defined process before tackling something more complex. For example, instead of trying to map an entire manufacturing operation, start with a specific work cell or operation. In an office environment, start with the accounts payable process instead of the entire financial management process. Sometimes, especially early on in a Lean transformation, it can be difficult to identify specific processes. I've seen way too many organizations take their first steps into value stream mapping by trying to map their entire organization. This generally results in mass confusion, disappointment, and walls covered with sticky notes.

Once again, it is best to perform the value stream mapping exercise at the process so it can be observed in real time. Traditionally, you use a large sheet of paper and draw the map by hand with a pen or pencil. If more than one person is involved, it may be easier to use a whiteboard or a wall with sticky notes. (You can use software too, but as I described earlier, I believe you learn more by writing by hand.)

The first step is to create the current state value stream map. Observe the process and detail each step in flowchart form. Traditional value stream mapping uses specific icons and symbols, which you can see on examples in the Resources section. Focus on material flow first, then look at information flow. Write down the average amount of time each step takes and how each step relates to the others. Be sure to observe multiple runs of the process so you can also note variations in the process and any issues that arise. Also, note the rate of customer demand so that you can calculate takt time as well as the total time the process takes.

Once everyone is satisfied that the value stream map accurately reflects the process, it is time to review, discuss, and envision ways to improve it. Ask yourself where waste is being generated, particularly in terms of time or idle materials and equipment. Determine which steps are value-added and which are non-value-added. (Think about "value" from the perspective of the customer.)

Remember that some steps may not be value-added from the perspective of the customer, but may still be required, such as paperwork required by regulations or additional testing the company is undertaking as part of a continuous project. You want the process flow rate to match to takt time driven by customer demand and make the process flow better to reduce waiting or transportation. Look for any bottlenecks and how can they be resolved. Remember the seven forms of waste and attempt to eliminate them.

From that discussion, create a new future state value stream map incorporating the ideas for improvement. While doing so, also create an action plan to change from the current state to the future state. Answer questions such as: What equipment needs to be moved? How does the process need to be rearranged? What visual controls will you use to monitor the new process? What is the timing and priority of these action items, and who is responsible? Document these required actions visually on an A3 report and monitor any changes you make via the daily accountability process that we will discuss later.

Improvement Kata

It is a mistake to look too far ahead. Only one link in the chain
of destiny can be handled at a time.
– Winston Churchill

Earlier, when discussing how to engage and lead people with respect, I described the coaching kata, a process that helps managers teach employees to approach performance improvement scientifically. The key is to help workers focus on a target condition and the steps to get there, by running what are effectively experiments in a PDCA cycle. This approach, known as improvement kata, teaches workers to adapt to changing conditions and to overcome unforeseen obstacles when trying to reach the target condition.

As with coaching kata, the first step of improvement kata is to set a target condition. The target condition is different than a goal in that it is the ultimate condition, i.e., what has to occur for the process to be successful. For example, if the customer demand is ten units each day, then that is the target condition. A goal—to produce six units, for example—may be a great improvement, but it might not achieve what the customer needs.

The kata method is based on moving forward one step at a time using small experiments, creating rapid, small improvements or rapid, small failures. You start by knowing what the actual condition (current state) is. Once you have the actual and target conditions, you observe the process and identify what obstacles are preventing you from achieving the target condition. These may be training, equipment, technology, human talent, facility, and so forth. Do not spend too much time prioritizing obstacles or attempting to gauge the relative impact of the obstacles.

From your list of obstacles, identify one that can potentially be improved, and run an experiment. What is the result? What have you learned? And what is the next step? The next step can be another small experiment building on the success or failure of the current experiment, or it can be more analysis of the current experiment. They key is to simply keep moving forward toward the target condition with rapid experiments.

Note how different the kata method is from traditional improvement projects. Traditional improvement projects create a detailed action plan, with every step of the march toward the goal mapped out. With improvement kata, the end point is the ultimate target condition and instead of worrying about all the steps of the plan, only the next obstacle is acted on. This can turn traditional project planning on its head, but the rapid experiments create ongoing forward movement and, perhaps most importantly, lots of new knowledge.

Daily Management and Accountability

The key to the Toyota Way and what makes Toyota stand out is not any of the individual elements…But what is important is having all the elements together as a system. It must be practiced every day in a very consistent manner, not in spurts.
– Taiichi Ohno

For a Lean transformation to be sustained, it must be practiced and supported each and every day. Too many organizations try to implement Lean tools without understanding and embracing the Lean philosophy. They review "Lean" improvements and practices only on a weekly, monthly, or even quarterly basis. To work, Lean must be a part of the daily management routine.

Daily management at a Lean organization has several components. It often begins early in the morning with a daily standup meeting. As I mentioned earlier, this was one of the few

Lean methods I had to dictate, because creating yet another meeting—let alone a daily meeting—is met with a lot of resistance! However, if run correctly, everyone soon realizes it is a very valuable meeting and it becomes self-sustaining.

Daily meetings generally start at the gemba and move up through the organization each morning, with a representative—typically the team leader, supervisor, or manager—attending the next-level-up meeting. At my previous company, the meetings started on the production floor at 6:30 a.m. and worked their way up to my executive team meeting at 8:30  a.m., which included a videoconference with our other two facilities. If a member couldn't be there, he or she was expected to send a representative. Having these substitutes present, plus the fact that the meetings were always open to anyone else in the company, helped grow the leadership capability of our entire company—again, showing respect for people.

The key to making the daily meeting successful was sticking with its primary purpose, which was to review any deviations from the plan. The meeting was not a general project or production review. As a result, the entire meeting, even at an executive level responsible for multiple facilities, only lasted between five and fifteen minutes (usually closer to five). However, the informa-

179

tion conveyed was extremely valuable and very timely, allowing us to address any problems quickly. With day-to-day issues identified and resolved quickly, most of the discussions at our weekly executive staff meetings became focused on long-term issues. With fewer issues to discuss, the executive meeting soon became a biweekly (and later monthly) event.

Each of our daily standup meetings had a very similar agenda:

- Safety issues (demonstrating respect for people right at the beginning)
- Celebration of any new successes: customers made happy, project completion, etc. (again, demonstrating respect for people with recognition)
- Notification of any incoming visitors (so we were prepared to show respect—including by not wearing jeans!)
- Customer issues
- Quality issues (deviation from the standard)
- Production issues (deviation from the plan)
- Round robin of all present, in case they have other issues
- Review of the Daily Accountability Board

The Daily Accountability Board was added after I left by my successor, Steve Kane. It was a large whiteboard with the day of the month written across the top and each executive staff member's name along the left side. The whiteboard, and our executive standup meeting, was in our de facto obeya room, which wasn't a room but a wide section of hallway that was open and visible to all, at all times. When issues were brought up during the standup meeting, members of the team took ownership of the issue and placed a sticky note on the board that included the date when the person committed to having it resolved.

When that day arrived, the person had to report on the status (there was no daily report until the date arrived) of the problem. If the task was complete, the sticky note was removed. If it wasn't complete, a red dot was added to the note for each day it was late, and if the date was rescheduled the dots stayed. This wasn't to overtly create a "strike" against the person, but was a visual indicator that we had somehow underestimated the time required. The delay could be due to workload, complexity, or other factors. Knowing what caused it helped us learn and improve.

In addition to daily standup meetings, other key components of daily management and accountability we used were leader standard work and the gemba walk, both discussed earlier. At my companies, all leaders were expected to have leader standard work. On our daily gemba walks, all leaders were expected to review visual management charts, visual controls such as andons, whiteboards with metrics and other information, and other executives' leader standard work. Examples of all of these are in the Resources section.

A New Take on Training

No one learns as much about a subject
as one who is forced to teach it.
– Peter F. Drucker

Imagine you were manufacturing a critical device needed to keep our country safe, when all of a sudden over 80% of your assembly team disappeared and you had to hire new people with no experience. What would you do?

This is exactly what happened during World War II, when most working-age men went off to fight the war. Factories making bombers, tanks, and other critical war equipment—not to mention goods and equipment needed for day-to-day use at home—lost their assembly teams. The wives of the soldiers took their place, but they lacked training or experience.

This shortage of skilled workers led to the adoption of a system known as Training Within Industry, or TWI. TWI was a way for companies to develop their workers' skills through on-the-job training. The U.S. Government War Production Board created the TWI Service to assist companies, and by the end of the war, over 1.6 million people in more than 16,000 factories had been trained and certified.

After the war, TWI was quickly forgotten in the United States. However, in Japan, the government, along with companies such as Toyota, adopted it to help rebuild the country's post-war manufacturing capability. Toyota leveraged TWI in its continuous improvement efforts, and many believe it played a part in their development of the standard work concept.

Only recently has TWI once again emerged on the Lean scene in the United States, and its use is now expanding into non-manufacturing organizations in the healthcare, government, and the general service industries.

TWI has three main components: Job Instruction (JI), which teaches instructors how to train employees faster; Job Methods (JM), which teaches employees how to analyze processes and suggest improvements; and Job Relations (JR), which teaches supervisors how to deal with employee issues in a humane and fair way.

Several other components were used sporadically, such as , Program Development (PD), Union Job Relations (UJR), problem solving (PS), and Discussion Leading (DL). They are not important for our discussion on improvement, so we'll focus primarily on the first two, Job Instruction (JI) and Job Methods (JM), as those are the two that are generally adopted in a TWI effort.

The purpose of Job Instruction training is to help the instructor understand every detail of the process. To prepare for JI training, instructors:

1. Break the process into the key steps.
2. Document the key points for each step.
3. Document the reasons behind why the step is important.

Once instructors complete this analysis, they start training others, using the following steps:

1. The instructor demonstrates each step of the process to the student, explaining the key points and reasons for each step.
2. The student performs the process step by step, with the instructor correcting any mistakes.
3. The student performs the process step by step again, this time explaining the key points for each one, with the instructor again correcting any mistakes.
4. The student performs the process step by step a third time, explaining both the key points and the reasons for each step. Once again, the instructor corrects any mistakes. Repeat until the instructor is confident the student understands the process.
5. The student then demonstrates the process again, the first time silently, the second time explaining the key points, and the third time explaining the key points and reasons.
6. The student performs the process alone, with a clear understanding that he or she can ask for assistance at any time without retribution. This demonstrates respect for people by creating a supportive, no-fear environment.

As you can see, the key to JI is repetition. Instructors repeat the training until it is clear the employee deeply understands the work process.

Once the worker understands the work, they can move on to Job Methods (JM) training. JM teaches employees how to break down and improve processes. The steps in JM are:

1. Break down the job into steps on a Job Breakdown Sheet.

Include material handling, machine time, and human time.

2. Question every detail of the job. This often uses the "5 W and 1 H" method:
   a. *Why* is it necessary?
   b. *What* is its purpose?
   c. *Where* should it be done?
   d. *When* should it be done?
   e. *Who* is qualified to do it?
   f. *How* is the best way to do it?
3. Develop the new method by eliminating steps, rearranging steps, and simplifying steps.
4. Propose the new method to the supervisor, test it, and then celebrate the accomplishment (when it works).

Both JI and JM involve breaking down the processes, although JM goes into more depth. Because of this, many organizations, like my previous company, use JM as one of their kaizen methods.

How could JI or JM change how you train people in your organization? How might they help the new employee onboarding process?

Reflection

I will take time to be alone today. I will take time to be quiet.
In this silence I will listen...and I will hear my answers.
– Ruth Fishel

One of my great pleasures is going for a walk on the six-mile-long and generally empty beach a couple blocks from my house. There's the remnant of a long-dormant (hopefully!) volcano at one end that is strangely humbling. A long walk in such a beautiful spot creates a connection between nature, my body, my mind, and God— a connection often never made while I'm buried in the chaos of normal life. It is a time for reflection and re-centering that allows me to contemplate many important questions as I walk:

How am I doing, mentally, spiritually, and physically? What am I grateful for? What do I need to forgive myself for? Am I on track to achieve my personal and professional goals? What countermeasures do I need to put in place? What new opportunities can I create? What should I do more or less of? What activities or thoughts should I stop? Regularly asking and answering those questions is critical for effective professional and personal leadership.

On a personal level, I have a fairly standardized reflection regime. Each evening I reflect on the day's activities, both personal and professional. If I didn't accomplish my Big Three goals, I try to understand why and put into place countermeasures to improve. I also take stock of how I am doing emotionally, spiritually, and physically.

At least once or twice a week, generally as part of my meditation practice, I walk on the beach and do a deeper reflection with myself, as described above. Once a month, I review my journal, looking for open action items and copying and consolidating them to a new page. The act of doing this sparks a conversation with myself about those action items. Are they still important? If so, why were they not accomplished? What can I do differently?

Each quarter, I try to get away for a couple days of solitude and a change of pace for reviewing and reflecting (*datsuzoku* and *seijaku*) on the year. Am I meeting my goals? What should I change?

Finally, once a year, generally around the end of the calendar year, I will go away on a peaceful vacation with my wife. During that time, both with her and while alone, I will do a final reflection on the year. I ask myself if I am holding true to my principles and values, what should change, and what goals I should set for the following year.

This type of individual reflection is valuable, and it is also very beneficial for professional teams to do a regular group reflection. In the Lean world, this is called hansei. I used to take my executive staff to an offsite meeting at least twice a year, generally at a local winery. We'd start by reviewing our core principles and values, determine if any adjustments needed to be made, then review our annual plans and goals. (Taking careful notes of these meetings was critical, because afterward, we would spend the rest of the afternoon partaking of the facility's best beverages, celebrating and getting to know each other.)

Effective personal leadership, requiring conscious individual reflection, is critical for effective professional leadership. Take some time alone, perhaps in the grandeur of nature, to humbly ask yourself some tough questions. Your responses to these questions will help you clarify your own goals and principles, allowing you to share them with others in your professional life and your personal life.

Celebrate Success

Celebrate the journey. It's not all about the destination.
Savor all of your successes, even the small ones.
– Dawn Gluskin

Finally, you made some improvements! Or, perhaps, you failed but learned something in the process. In both cases, you should celebrate with your team. This is respecting the people that made it happen.

A celebration can be as easy as saying a few words in private or at the morning standup meeting. It can also be a lunch or a gift. Since you are now mindful and connected to your team and understand their needs and desires (and your own), you can design the appropriate celebration. At my last company, one of the favorite ways we celebrated was to present successes at the quarterly continuous improvement meeting. Improvements large and small were presented, shared, celebrated, and learned from. As I mentioned earlier, after a morning of hansei reflection, my executive staff would spend the afternoons of our quarterly executive offsite retreat, usually held at a nearby winery, enjoying the products of that location and each other's company.

Showing appreciation can be very powerful and, unfortunately, is often overlooked. A simple word of thanks to an individual, team, or entire organization is very motivational. Say it often, but ensure it is also special. Specifically mention the activity, project, or behavior that is worthy of the thanks. Finally, make it timely by delivering it within a day after the occurrence that warranted the thanks. Be mindful of individual and team dynamics, tailoring the message and delivery method appropriately. When you show appreciation this way, you build stronger relationships, create a positive atmosphere, and improve the team spirit within your organization.

(Thank you for making it this far through this book! Congratulations! Now let's grow even further.)

Part Eight - Grow

Through learning we grow, becoming more than we were before,
and in that sense learning is unselfish, because it results in the
transformation of what we were before, a setting aside of the old self
in favor of a more complex one.
– Mihaly Csíkszentmihályi

We've covered a lot already. You've learned how to connect with who you really are, work productively, lead your team, clarify your plan, simplify your environment, and create continuous improvement. But the journey doesn't end there. You must continue to grow and expand your horizons. You have so much potential!

Key Points in this Section
- We all are continually evolving.
- Work to add new knowledge and perspectives, mindfully challenging your comfort zone and biases.
- Challenge your comfort zone by exploring out of the box and doing, learning, or visiting something radically different.
- Create your own unique path in life.
- Life is like a painting: you add experiences and knowledge and combine them into art.

Evolution

*Once, after a particularly claustrophobic, stressful and
over-populated time when there hadn't been air or space to escape
to, suddenly, for a few days, I was alone. It was like emigrating to
another planet (in fact I was at home). Who was this person I was
living with, this strange, this reasonable, serene foreigner in the
house: a becalmed woman who spent her time inwardly humming?*
– Mirabel Osler

After meditating and focusing inward for several weeks
(or even months), you may realize something: you aren't who
you thought you were. This moment of understanding your true
nature, known as *kensho* in the Zen realm, can be a bit terrifying.
What if I told you that your understanding of who you are would
continue to evolve and change?

This understanding can be very powerful from both
personal and professional leadership perspectives. Your confidence in your decisions and your intuition will increase. You will
feel and be seen as more authentic. Life will be more satisfying.

Understanding who you are helps you identify your
purpose, and knowing your purpose enables you to focus your
efforts on improvement. Embrace and think about the unfolding
revelation of your true nature. How does it change your leadership
style, your decisions, your commitment to your family, and your
career choices? Allow and relish those changes.

Continue to Learn

Learning is not compulsory...neither is survival.
– W. Edwards Deming

Many, if not most people go to school and college, and then, when they are finished, rarely open another book (at least one with big words in it). They may continue to grow their skills and knowledge through experience, but this is the slow boat to improvement.

Over the years, I've found that the primary predictor of executive leadership competency is the desire to seek, learn, analyze, distill, and share new knowledge. It doesn't necessarily have to be within the leader's current field or competency, nor does it have to be strictly via reading books. There are multiple pathways to new knowledge, including online courses, magazines, and workshops.

Gaining new knowledge can also mean gaining new perspectives. As I discussed earlier, in a world of multiple sources of information, it is very easy to succumb to confirmation bias and only embrace information that fits our existing perspective. In reality, there is almost always some truth in every perspective. Challenge yourself to mindfully look at other perspectives on political, scientific, or social issues in an unbiased manner. You may not change your mind, but you will grow and your positions will be more authentic.

I try to read one fiction and one non-fiction book each month, which is sometimes difficult with my schedule. The non-fiction books, generally business-related, challenge me intellectually. The fiction, often science fiction or action thrillers, challenge my imagination. Each morning, I read *The Wall Street Journal* on my iPad, forwarding articles to friends and family that I find interesting. I purposely try to read articles from different political sources instead of only the ones that agree with my perspectives. I try to continually evaluate my perspectives, think about where bias is setting in and develop countermeasures to overcome the bias.

Think about your own pursuit of knowledge. What have you learned recently? What do you want or need to learn this year? How will you do it? What will you do with the new knowledge? How does it fit in with your new self-awareness? How will you encourage and provide opportunities for your team to learn?

Do Something Different

Unless you try to do something beyond what you have already mastered, you will never grow.
– Ralph Waldo Emerson

Acquiring new knowledge and perspectives helps you grow within your general area of comfort or interest. To really grow, you need to stretch yourself outside of that comfort zone by learning or experiencing something completely different. In addition to acquiring the new skill, knowledge, or experience, you also create confidence in your ability to break boundaries. This can help you awaken to your true meaning.

A couple years ago, I came across an article by Heather Kelly on CNN.com ("Mark Zuckerberg's Bizarre New Self-Improvement

Goal") about how Facebook's Mark Zuckerberg sets an annual "challenge" goal:

> Every year, the Facebook CEO sets some sort of challenge for himself. In 2009, he vowed to wear a tie to work every day to show he was serious about Facebook's growth (and possibly get a break from the signature T-shirt and hoodie he wears to every public event). In 2010, he tried to learn Mandarin.
>
> The annual challenges sometimes make headlines, most famously in 2011 when Zuck vowed to eat animals only if he had killed them himself. That pronouncement led to a mixture of backlash and praise from animal-rights activists.
>
> This year [2012], the famously introverted Zuckerberg is seeking out more conversations with actual humans.

Seeking out more human interaction as a goal seems a bit odd until you think about the world that the young founder of Facebook lives in: a rarified air of groupies, yes-men, analysts, and press types. Interacting with "actual humans" is probably a challenge. Why is that bizarre? I applaud him for it. In 2013, Zuckerberg's goal was to meet someone new every day; in 2014, he challenged himself to write one thank you note each day; and in 2015, he read a new book every other week.

A key outcome to these challenges is that he learns something new and (often) unexpected. Trying to learn Mandarin taught him that he didn't listen well, and a year of killing animals made him consider becoming vegetarian. Zuckerberg's 2012 goal, to converse with humans, helped him understand the personal side of immigration issues.

The reason Zuckerberg's "bizarre" goals resonated with me is because I have had similar goals for well over twenty years. At first they weren't true goals—they were just something fun to do. But for the last decade or more, the goals have been formal, with a process for identifying, executing and reviewing progress.

Over the past couple decades, I learned to scuba dive, windsurf, and code HTML by hand. I wrote a book, rebuilt a yellow 1973 Triumph Spitfire, became a vegetarian (rather, a "pesca-terian"), skied in five different European countries over six days, started a blog, and ran a full marathon. Toward the end  of each year, I identify something to try that is different, unique, or challenging, and develop a plan to dive into it. During the next year, I execute, reflect, and adjust based on my observations. Sound familiar? Plan, do, study, act.

In 2012, my goal was to leave a great job as president of a medical device company and take more control of my life. I notified the board in January, executed a transition plan for myself and the company, and, like a skydiver jumping out of a perfectly good airplane, left full-time secure employment on December 31st. I'm loving it, and the move also created positive secondary effects for the company: a great new Lean leader was developed to replace me and the company got a fresh infusion of Lean energy.

One of my other recent goals—related to this book—was to learn about and understand Buddhism, something I'd bumped into during my trips to Asia and also while living in California. I read books about it, talked to a lot of people, and in a sense, went to the gemba by spending a few weeks in Bhutan and Nepal. I learned about Zen's history, how it evolved and split into the Theravada and Mahayana traditions, how Mahayana then evolved into Pure Land, Tibetan, and the Zen tradition that's increasingly popular in the West. What I learned changed how I understood myself.

My goal this year is to read an important work of literature from each of the major ethnic groups or cultures: Latin American, Chinese, Indian, African, and so forth. My annual exploration takes me down some interesting and often unexpected paths, teaching me new thoughts, knowledge, or activities.

The point is that many people say they "think outside the box" but most do not actually explore outside the box. Relatively few people live with an open mind, and even fewer create goals to stretch themselves. Most people find it very difficult to put processes and hansei in place (Zuckerberg apparently does) because it is easier to talk than to act.

I can't claim credit for knowingly thinking outside the box, especially initially. I sort of fell into doing it. But trying new things has broadened my perspectives by challenging my old perceptions and beliefs. It has deepened my understanding of the world we live in and taken me to interesting places—both physical and spiritual—that I previously wasn't even aware of.

How will you explore out of the box next year? Perhaps

more importantly, how will you ensure you actually do it, and why?

Explore the World

*As often as possible, go someplace you've never been before.
Experience new places and new things. You might find yourself with
someone or somewhere that makes you much happier than your
previous circumstance. The Earth is so vast with unique and
beautiful places, why wouldn't you want to go explore them?*
– Dalai Lama

My annual "do something different" goal is coupled with another goal my wife and I have had for the past decade: to visit two new countries each year. We've blown that one out of the box, having traveled to more than sixty new countries during that time.

Today, with each country I visit, I learn something new and unexpected that changes my perceptions, challenges my biases, and adds to my worldview. In Japan, I learned about a culture steeped in respect for family and fellow citizens. In India, I discovered a people that were incredibly dedicated and industrious, but hampered by lack of infrastructure. In Morocco, I experienced a very peaceful and friendly side of Islam that runs counter to what many believe about it. In Tanzania, I saw firsthand the infrastructure, health, and social problems associated with hyper-growth. It's not just me that gains from visiting other cultures. Many years ago, Howard Schultz was traveling around Europe and was drawn to the coffee shops. When he returned, he channeled all his energy into recreating his experiences there, and Starbucks was born.

Because I learn so much when I travel, I find it very scary how many folks in the U.S. haven't been outside of the country (or perhaps have only traveled to Mexico and Canada). As a result, they have a worldview driven purely by news sound bites and by the biases of their friends with similarly narrow views.

I thank my parents for giving me the travel bug. In the early '70s, with two young kids, Dad quit a great job (perhaps it runs in the family?) and took our family to live in Peru—a military dictatorship at the time—to work for the Peace Corps. Eighteen months later, the Peace Corps was kicked out of the country for supposedly being a front for the CIA. When that happened, my father switched to working for the US State Department and we stayed for another six years (basically all of my high school years).

At the time, there were nearly 40,000 Americans in Peru. Most worked for the oil and mining companies, which gave them a significantly higher economic status than the families who worked for the Peace Corps. This was not the best situation for an impressionable kid, but it was humbling in hindsight.

Life in Peru was much different than life in the U.S. The military dictatorship was very careful about controlling the flow of information between Peru and the outside world. Technological limitations also made communication outside of Peru difficult. I remember waiting a month for Time magazine to arrive, and having to schedule phone calls back to the U.S. days in advance. Although there was a large and very good American School where we lived, going out in the evenings wasn't something you did as a school kid.

While I didn't always like living in Peru, my parents made

sure I at least got a cultural education out of the experience. They took my sister and me, usually kicking and screaming, to count-less museums and cultural events. I'm now thankful they did. We

visited Machu Picchu a number of times. We took a month off one summer and drove our mustard Chevy Suburban south through Chile, across Argentina, and then north through Paraguay, Brazil,  and Bolivia. We also visited Ecuador, Colombia, and Venezu-ela. We crossed rivers on railroad bridges, hoping a train wasn't coming, drove in the rain over some incredibly narrow, unpaved roads carved into mountains (again, praying no one was coming), and were stopped by cops asking for immediate payment in cash for not having the "mandatory" fire extinguisher in our car. Those were crazy, scary days, but I miss them.

I understand there can be a significant financial barrier to traveling, but when possible, you should invest the time and money in seeing other parts of the world. The benefits are too great not to. If possible, go places that have very different cultures than your own, for that's where you'll learn the most. Material goods have a finite life. Experiences last—and have impact—forever.

When you visit, be sure to take the time to see life outside the tourist areas, in addition to the usual monuments and muse-ums. My wife and I always ask for tours of regular neighborhoods and other non-touristy areas, and we will often spend a day giving back at orphanages or shelters. One Christmas we brought and handed out gifts at a women's shelter in a dangerous part of Colon, Panama. The experience was both humbling and very meaningful, and will stick with us for the rest of our lives.

Find Your Unique Path

Living is the constant adjustment of thought to life and life to thought in such a way that we are always growing, always experiencing new things in the old and old things in the new. Thus life is always new.
– Thomas Merton

I was rather surprised when Pope Francis mentioned Thomas Merton, a Catholic monk, philosopher, and author, in his address to Congress during the pope's visit to the United States in 2015. I first came across Merton's work during my deep dive into Buddhism a few years back, and his *Thoughts in Solitude* is one of my favorite books. Merton is a controversial figure in the Catholic church, because in addition to being a priest, he was also a student of Zen Buddhism. Hence, it was remarkable that Pope Francis lauded Merton, who once said: "I see no contradiction between Buddhism and Christianity. I intend to become as good a Buddhist as I can."

Driving Merton's interest in Zen was his belief that most Christian traditions had become so focused on ritual and dogma that they had forgotten about the quest for understanding and having a true personal relationship with the ultimate source of

201

that knowledge. In both his writing and his own spiritual journey, Merton embraced the fundamental Buddhist concept that there is no one perfect path to enlightenment or salvation, and that each of us has to understand ourselves before creating our own unique journey. This idea does conflict with many Christian (especially Catholic) traditions, but not all of them.

In 2015, my annual goal was to dive deeply into the history of the Bible, partly to assuage some family members concerned about my foray into Buddhism. I read about palace intrigue at the Vatican and in the early Church, mysterious sailors carrying fragments of scriptures to faraway lands, scribes with hidden agendas, and archeological finds that both confirmed and denied prior sets of beliefs. It was an enlightening experience.

One of the subjects that came up in my research was the Gnostics. For most of the current era, the Gnostics were more commonly known as "those crazy Gnostics." They had strange rituals and beliefs, only loosely associated with Christianity, which is why the early Vatican councils quickly discarded their scriptures and did not include them in the traditional Biblical canon. Then, in 1945, the Nag Hammadi texts were found and translated (interestingly, with financial support from none other than the noted psychiatrist, Carl Jung). The new texts supported some of earliest-known manuscripts that had been deemed too controversial by the early church to use in the Bible. They described a spiritual belief system far more aligned with traditional Christianity than originally thought, although there were still differences.

One of the major differences was that Gnostics did not insist everyone must believe as they did. To the Gnostics, faith was an inner experience (the same as in classical Christianity), but it did not have to be the same for everyone, as long as it was grounded in individual investigation, introspection, reflection, and circumstance instead of ritual. In other words, faith is a dynamic process of seeking truth, not arrogantly declaring it. Sound familiar?

Almost daily, I come across articles, questions, and comments about the "true path" to Lean and the supposedly correct sequence of methods required to accomplish a transformation. This misconception, along with not understanding the respect for humanity pillar, is what causes most Lean failures.

Like the spiritual journeys of Buddhists, Gnostics, and Christians like Thomas Merton, when you are on your own journey, you must first seek to learn, understand, contemplate, and reflect on your circumstances and beliefs. Only then can you apply what makes sense to create your own path. Don't simply accept what others say or copy what others do.

Life as Art

Life is pure adventure, and the sooner we realize that,
the quicker we will be able to treat life as art.
– Maya Angelou

Life is a canvas, shaped by what is in your soul, the environment you are in, your decisions, and your interactions with others. Your life is an individual, unique work of art. How can you change what's on that canvas, the art of you? Here are some suggestions:

- Slow down. Take the time to experience all aspects of your life.
- Be present. Truly use all of your five senses. In fact, when sitting, purposely go through all your five senses and experience what they are telling you.
- Explore. Add new experiences and knowledge to the canvas. Take risks.
- Synthesize. Just as an artist mixes paints and even media, think about how the various aspects of your life are mixing together.

When I first started painting my canvas, I thought I would be a fireman or superhero, but over time this changed to physicist, then chemical engineer. I went from manufacturing to executive management to being the cofounder of an e-learning startup. I started out fairly conservative, then as I witnessed and reflected on the experiences of myself and others, I evolved into a far more complex sociopolitical individual. As I began to learn and explore, I experimented with and adopted intellectual and spiritual frameworks that made sense and were relevant to my situation. My time growing up in South America eventually led me to visit and experience more than sixty countries, and after more than fifty years, these experiences have given my canvas many complex layers.

What will you add to your canvas today? This year? What will your life's canvas eventually look like? Become aware, reflect on your personal and professional leadership life, and improve every day. Add depth, color, and texture to your painting. Make it a work of art you can be proud of.

Resources

Online resources, including template downloads and links to referenced books, are at http://www.thesimpleleader.com

Recommended books to explore concepts in more detail

Building the Fit Organization – Daniel Markovitz

The Culture of Kaizen – Jon Miller

Discover Your True North – by Bill George

Drive: The Surprising Truth About What Motivates Us – Dan Pink

Essentialism: The Disciplined Pursuit of Less – Gregory McKeown

A Factory of One – Daniel Markovitz

The Five Dysfunctions of a Team – Patrick Lencioni

Humble Inquiry: The Gentle Art of Asking Instead of Telling – Edgar Schein

Joy, Inc. – Richard Sheridan

The Laws of Subtraction – Matthew May

Lean Health – Paul Akers

Lead with Respect – Michael Ballé

The Lean Manager – Michael Ballé

The Lost Art of Walking – Geoff Nicholson

The Outstanding Organization – Karen Martin

The Power of Habit: Why We Do What We Do in Life and Business – Charles Duhigg

The Shibumi Strategy – Matthew May

Thoughts in Solitude – Thomas Merton

Toyota Kata – Mike Roether

True North – Bill George

205

Zen Mind, Beginner's Mind – Shunryu Suzuki

About the Author

Kevin Meyer has over thirty years of executive leadership, operations, engineering, and Lean transformation experience in the medical device, automotive lighting, and telecom photonics equipment industries.

He is currently partner and co-founder of Gemba Academy, which provides Lean and Six Sigma training videos to over 2,000 companies worldwide. He sits on the boards of two startup technology companies and works with other startups as a partner in SLO Seed Ventures.

Previously, Kevin was President of Specialty Silicone Fabricators, a contract manufacturer of silicone components for the medical device industry. He co-founded a contract manufacturing company, Agilonics, turned around a hyper-growth telecom photonics operation of Newport Corporation, and held various engineering and operations management positions at Abbott Laboratories and Sylvania.

Kevin has a BS in Chemical Engineering from Rensselaer Polytechnic Institute and resides in Morro Bay, California.

To contact Kevin or learn more, please visit http://www.kevinmeyer.com.

Index

Made in the USA
Lexington, KY
09 December 2016